Jolyon Simmonds
Hampstead, NW.3
1 July 1988.

CRUISING THE SAHARA

CRUISING THE SAHARA

Gerard Morgan-Grenville

with plates,
text illustrations and maps

DAVID & CHARLES
NEWTON ABBOT   LONDON
NORTH POMFRET (VT) VANCOUVER

To all those who seek the unknown: not to conquer and despoil
but, through understanding, to respect and protect.

0 7153 6467 7

Set in 11 on 13pt Baskerville
and printed in Great Britain
by The Devonshire Press Limited Torquay
for David & Charles (Holdings) Limited
South Devon House Newton Abbot Devon

Published in the United States of America
by David & Charles Inc North Pomfret
Vermont 05053 USA

Published in Canada
by Douglas David & Charles Limited
3645 McKechnie Drive, West Vancouver BC

Contents

Contents

Contents

Illustrations

Illustrations

Introduction

Saharan travel is, for many, a journey of romantic exploration contained within the imagination: a voyage to a Great Beyond. The Sahara is a geographical and historical mystery, a vastness which is permanently out of focus and of which the blurred edges merge hazily with the North African periphery. In the mind's eye we build images of our own Sahara: foreign legionnaires paraded before their desert fort, murderous Tuareg tribesmen armed with antique muskets mounting a camel charge, sun-crazed men in shorts and topee staggering drunkenly towards a fatal mirage, endless rippled dunes of scorching soft sand rendering each short step a terrible exertion, whitened bones on yellow sand, swarming flies that drive you insane, scorpions beneath every stone, the legendary Timbuktu forbidding entry to the infidel, camel caravans padding silently through the moonlight in hopeless search of wells which have not dried.

So firmly do many of us cling to our fantasies that we find it hard to realise that there is another Sahara as alluring as ours is frightening.

This is the real Sahara: the greatest desert on earth and yours almost for the asking. To explore its expanse is to become acquainted with the surface of the moon or the bed of the oceans. It is to experience a solitude and tranquillity that is unknown in Europe. It is to see the earth on the day of Creation, in all its nakedness. To stand on virgin desert beneath stars of incredible brightness, in a silence which is absolute, is to undergo a profound experience. To stare across golden sand, under the blue hemisphere of each day toward the rose-coloured hills of a distant horizon, or to contemplate the voluptuous curves of rising dunes, or the sudden emerald of a verdant oasis, is to be recharged spiritually. Had you thought of a Sahara of flowers, or of birds that are ludicrously tame? Of rocks carved by the wind with such supernatural skill as to make the works of abstract sculptors seem sadly contrived? Of combing the markets for fragrant spices at ridiculously low prices? Or of simply making off toward the horizon to stand where perhaps no man has ever stood before?

Lest you think that I romanticise the desert I will be more objective. When the winter fogs or cold spring winds afflict our island, this great desert enjoys the best weather of a British July. And not just one day isolated between others of wind or rain, but a whole string, each and every one predictably fine, clear and hot. Even in March you may eat fresh pineapple, mangoes or strawberries. Depending where you are, you may see gazelle or crocodile. You may climb peaks that are unnamed and unclimbed, or enter a country with no marked boundaries and drive for two days to reach a frontier post.

You can join the relatively few to see the greatest rock paintings in the world, works of magnificent simplicity and astonishing elegance, or see some of the greatest Roman ruins. Mud-built forts of great architectural beauty exist in profusion. Two people may stand in the North African desert separated by 3,000 miles of emptiness without a single metalled road between them. You can be below sea-level or 11,000ft above it. You may travel 500 miles across open desert and not see a living soul or you can move along smooth tarmac from luxury hotel to luxury hotel.

Whatever your reasons for travel, you can be assured that this, the most magnificent of all deserts, contains variety enough for all, rich or poor, old or young. Its fringes are accessible by car, bus or train and its interior by truck, four-wheel drive vehicle or camel.

Britain is one of the most densely populated countries on

earth. The effects of this overcrowding impinge on us from all directions and affect our bodily and mental well-being. We are almost never out of the sight, sound or smell of traffic, aircraft and the Great Industrial Machine. What better reason, therefore, to visit the loneliest place on earth? It is a restorative to mind and body. You will see the world in a new perspective. You will return a changed being, liberated in spirit and the Sahara will have you in its grip.

I

The Sahara

The name Sahara, derived from the Arabic word *Sahra*, meaning empty, is a loose geographical term applied to the great north African desert stretching from the Atlantic in the west to the Red Sea in the east.

It has no precise boundaries and consequently its area is estimated variously from 2½ to 3½ million square miles—the difference being equivalent to an area twenty times the size of England. Furthermore, this great desert—some six times larger than any other desert on earth—is divided into several adjacent deserts, of which by far the largest is the Sahara proper. It is this last with which the book is concerned, an area bounded to the east by the fifteenth parallel as far south as Lake Chad and to the south by a line from Lake Chad to Dakar on the Atlantic coast which then forms the western boundary, meeting up with the western end of the Atlas range: in other words, the western half of the north African desert. To the east of this region are the Libyan desert (which is mainly in Egypt and Sudan), the Arabian desert (which is in Egypt) and the Western Desert (which is in the east, in Egypt).

The entire area is about the same as that of the United States; it is 3,200 miles wide (at latitude 19°N) and at its broadest 1,500 miles (at 10°E); at its highest some 11,200ft and at its lowest over 400ft below sea-level. Only a sixth of the desert is covered by sand dunes (*erg*), a large part is characterised by rocky plateaux (*hamada*), or gravel plains (*reg*), and these are often channelled or deeply gouged by the action of water. Such river beds (*wadi*), are normally dry. The chief characteristics of the Sahara are its extreme aridity and its periods of intense heat.

Geologically the Sahara is a Pre-Cambrian shield composed of granite, mica, schist, gneiss, and quartz. Much of the Sahara represents the remains of a huge mountain range which has repeatedly sunk beneath the sea and this accounts for the numerous layers of sandstone, limestone and schist. Between the Tertiary and the Quaternary Era a volcanic folding process gave rise to such massives as the Hoggar, Aïr, Tibesti and Ajjer. Of the volcanoes it is mainly the pipes which are visible —huge cones of rubble surmounted by a cylindrical plug.

It was in the Quaternary Era that the great river valleys were formed. The low lying Chad area was beneath an inland sea while the large depressions (*shott*) in Algeria and Tunis were connected to the Mediterranean in the area of Gabès. The rock erosion caused by the formation of these river valleys is believed to account for the vast masses of sand which have been formed by the wind into the huge sand seas which, with their waves of dunes, are an effective barrier to travel.

Dunes are of several types. Some run with the prevailing wind, others at right angles to it. There are 'isolated' dunes which move perhaps an inch a day and there are the static dunes of the sand seas which seem hardly to move at all over the centuries. Dunes are rarely more than 400ft in height.

During the formation of the Sahara this vast land mass underwent powerful climatic alterations which characterised successive epochs. Although since the beginning of recorded history the climate seems to have changed very little, it is probable that a few thousand years before—perhaps 10,000 to 5,000 BC—the desert was a kind of tropical jungle. Prehistorians hold conflicting views on the nature of the Sahara during this period, but in support of the view of a green Sahara we have the numerous rock *graffiti* and paintings (which show animals now associated with tropical regions) and the remains of gigantic herbivorous mastodons which required the foliage of an entire tree for a single snack.

The population of the Sahara is about 2 million and, apart from the polar regions, it is the least populated area on earth: one head of population to the square mile (compared to 600 in the United Kingdom). Ethnically the population is very mixed and the endless bloody confrontations which have punctuated Saharan history are reflected in this diverse distribution of peoples and languages. In a rather dangerous oversimplification it may be said that in the west are Moors, to the north are Berbers, to the east Arabs, to the south Negroes and all over the centre the nomadic Tuareg, of whom more is said later.

The languages spoken (and their numerous dialects) include Arabic, Berber, Kanuri, Hausa and Tamaskek but the *lingua franca* for the white man is French.

Saharan history is totally absorbing. Unfortunately only the briefest synopsis can be allowed here but intending travellers should equip themselves with some literature on the subject. Some suggestions are made in Appendix H. We have already mentioned the speculative nature of Saharan pre-history and the surviving relics. In about 1200 BC the Phoenicians invaded North Africa and about a thousand years later (149 BC) the Romans landed at Carthage and conquered the whole of North Africa. They set up a highly efficient colonial empire in Mauretania (Algeria and Morocco), Numidia (Tunisia), Tripolitania (Libya) and Egypt. This entire area was policed and administered by a garrison of little more than ten thousand men who were responsible also for the immense constructional works, roads, water supplies, vineyards, temples, cities and forts, the ruins of which are still greatly in evidence.

Patrols were sent deep into the Sahara, possibly across it, and it was certainly better known to the Romans and to the Greek geographers than to the Europeans of 150 years ago. After the collapse of the Roman Empire the Vandals swept across the desert, giving way in the seventh century AD to the first of the Arab invasions. With them the Arabs brought the Mohammedan religion which replaced a partially established Christianity and which provided the main limitations to the subsequent development of Saharan history for the following thousand years.

The Arab conquest advanced nothing except the cause of Islam. The march of civilisation was paralysed by the fatalistic attitude of Mohammedans. The Moors in the west made some exploration and in the sixteenth century Leo Africanus wrote *A History and Description of Africa* which was, errors and all, used as the definitive work on the subject until, in the late eighteenth century, the first of the European explorers actually went to raise the curtain.

The stories of these early expeditions—mainly British at first, and then French and German—present an almost incredible account of difficulties, disease, deprivation, danger and death. Yet the courage and faith of the participants and the modest and objective manner of their reports is little less than inspirational. Names of expedition leaders that span an eighty-year period include those of Major Houghton, Frederick Hornemann, Mungo Park, Ritchie-Lyon, Oudney, Clapperton, Major Laing, Réné Caillé, Dr Davidson, Barth, Duveyrier, Miss Tinne, Dr Nachtigal—all but four dying or being murdered in the attempt. The great goal for many of these expeditions was Timbuktu. The fanaticism of the Moslems caused many of these men to disguise themselves accordingly—a process which could take years to perfect. The expeditions were dogged by lack of adequate finance, lack of medical knowledge and by the treachery of the Tuareg. The first European crossing of the Sahara east to west was in 1801 (Hornemann) and north to south in 1826 (Major Laing).

It was not only the expeditionaries who died. Then, as now, the absence of water killed off the ill-prepared. Entire caravans perished with as many as 2,000 men and 1,800 camels. The

Page 17
**METHODS
OF
SAHARAN
TRAVEL**
1 The hard
way—a party
exploring
on foot
2 The easy
way—for
travelling
trackless
mountains
such as the
Tassili it is
hard to
improve on
the donkey

Page 18 METHODS OF SAHARAN TRAVEL
3 Sand-yacht driven by M Bloit in the trans-Saharan sand-yacht race
4 Camel laden for short excursion

horrible fate of the slaves, the terrible sufferings of the salt miners and the bandit killers made the Sahara a bad risk to life for man and beast.

The great African land-snatching operation led by the European powers toward the end of the last century is, of course, recent history. In terms of square miles the French were easy winners with some four million, nearly twice that of the British and four times that of the German grabbers. The French 'area of influence' included the Sahara. An entire army failed to secure for the French the stability which the 'pacification' of Saharan natives was intended to achieve. But the French continued exploring and mapping the desert and, for a period, made it safe to travellers, though at the same time they discouraged foreign explorers by one means or another. Names that will long be remembered from the period of French occupation include those of Colonel Flatters whose extraordinary and tragic expedition was intended to survey a route for the still uncompleted trans-Saharan railway. General Laperrine crossed the Sahara eleven times on camel or on foot and created the Camel Corps (whose members lived the simple life of the nomads) and succeeded in swiftly patrolling vast areas in peace and friendship with the natives. He also organised the first motor convoys to the central Sahara and the first trans-Saharan air crossing in which he lost his life. The Hoggar Mountains' hermit, Lieutenant the Viscount de Foucauld, was the most famous of the White Fathers missionaries; he was murdered by the Tuareg in 1916.

In terms of trans-Saharan cruising, the end of a chapter came in 1923 when André Citröen's convoy of six tracked vehicles made the crossing from Tunis to Timbuktu in thirty days, without particular incident. It not only showed the world that the Sahara could now be travelled with speed and some comfort, but it also meant the approaching end of the camel as the ship of the desert.

Even the briefest notes about Saharan history would be incomplete without reference to the French Foreign Legion whose 'Beau Geste' forts are still such a feature in remote places. They were perhaps the last colonial fortresses to be built in the old style—crenellated walls and massive gates; inside, the barrack rooms around a courtyard; above, the embrasured walls and firing platforms. Many of these forts today stand empty, the great gates swinging in the wind. But in earlier times they were the scene not only of continual siege but also of the bestial life lived by the Foreign Legion soldiery. Though officered almost exclusively by the cream of the French officer-corps, the other ranks were composed of foreign—mainly German—deserters, murderers, thieves, swindlers and assorted fugitives from the law of their respective countries. To this rabble was added a German discipline which brutalised the legionaries into becoming automata. The story of the *Légion Etrangère* is not a pretty one. But today in their isolation and collapse these deserted bastions seem compellingly romantic.

The history of Saharan exploration and exploitation is over-laid with the history of the slave trade. The Arabs developed the business of capturing, driving and selling slaves, and from the end of the Middle Ages until the beginning of this century it became a vast and extremely lucrative trade. Slaves were exported during the 'boom' years at a rate of 100,000 a year. The total export of slaves to all destinations since the beginning of the sixteenth century was not less than 12 million. For every slave delivered alive at least one other died *en route* and some estimates put the figure as high as ten. The manner in which these slave caravans were flogged across the burning sand con-stitutes one of the worst chapters in the history of mankind. The main trans-Saharan slave routes are illustrated on page 52.

These routes were, and still are, littered with the bones of man and animal: it was said to be possible, on occasion, to find your way across the Sahara by following the stench of decaying corpses. The slave trade still exists but at only a fraction of its former volume, the 'difficulties' presented by official attitudes having tended to price the goods out of the market.

A word on the Tuareg—the race with which the desert traveller will probably have more contact than any other. The briefest acquaintance will suffice to convince the European that the Tuareg, nomadic, poor and disorganised though they are, possess qualities of durability, dignity and hospitality that are largely lost in our civilisation. Furthermore they are tall and strikingly handsome. Dressed in their sky-blue cloaks, their eyes alone visible between their headscarves (*shesh*) and veils (*litham*), the Tuareg are singularly imposing. No one knows for certain from where they come but it is a popular theory that they are the descendents of the Garamantians who ruled the area of Tripolitania in classical times. The Tuareg were lords of the desert, feared by all and sundry. The nobles were professional bandits and this expertise has not been entirely abandoned with their 'pacification'. They hold in contempt such activities as land husbandry and delegate such work to their Haratin slaves. Otherwise their economy is 'camelline' and in an age in which the Saharan caravan is in a state of collapse, it is obvious that the day of the Tuareg is over. But nothing pathetic is discernible in these ancient warriors who today roam the desert exactly as they did in Roman times. Their provision for a desert voyage remains a goatskin of meal and another of water, together with a small quantity of dates. Each man still carries a sword or a dagger and, on occasion, a shield. Their language is Tamashek, widely spoken but rarely written due to the extreme difficulty of writing the non-directional *T'ifinagh* script.

The new feature in the desert is oil. Politically it is of the utmost significance, but the oilmen live in a world apart from the desert traveller—fenced off, air conditioned, supplied with every luxury and in continual communication with the outside world. To the traveller, however, the Sahara is very much as it always has been.

In travelling the Sahara you are, generally speaking, in the land of the Arab; it is a mistake to feel that behaviour and customs will be European in character. It is wise to be very patient with the police and those in any position of authority. Wide allowances should be made for the very real differences which exist and a generous judgement made of the Arab system of life. If they appear slothful, incompetent and grasping, reflect briefly on their history, their poverty, their religion and the unyielding climate: these are among the determinant influences on their philosophy. I think it is an excusable generalisation to say that all Arabs have an insatiable appetite for gifts. They ask (particularly the women and children) for *cadeaux* persistently and unashamedly. The request, with the oft repeated 'please' (*baraka*), is shouted with apparent menace; if you offer, for example, a cigarette, do not be surprised if you lose the packet and receive a request for another.

Lastly, you should know that these same avaricious people can also be the soul of generosity. They have an equally pronounced sense of hospitality, like the Tuareg. They will not leave you to die of thirst in the desert if they can possibly help it. Similarly, it behoves you to offer what help you can to those you may encounter in need. Never pass a stranded vehicle without seeing if help is wanted.

2

Methods of Cruising the Desert

Your choice of 'where' will depend on your decision about 'how'. If, for instance, your decision as to *how* to travel is in favour of a bicycle, it is unlikely that you will decide that *where* you want to go is Timbuktu. *How* to travel will in turn depend on your spirit of adventure, your financial resources and the time available—all of which must be assessed by you; my only general advice is to avoid the mistake nearly every traveller makes, of trying to see too much: the less you see, the more you will remember, certainly the more you will enjoy it.

It is a fact that the desert exerts a powerful influence on many people and their first visit is seldom their last. But just in case you do not fall under the spell, it may be wise to start gently—putting one toe in the pool, so to speak, before throwing yourself in. Another consideration is whether you prefer to be on your own, with a party of friends, or with a larger mixed party of people whom you may not know.

So, with these points in mind, you may wish to consider the following methods, starting with 'private' transport. Dividing this into two main groups, automotive and non-automotive, I will start with the latter.

The prime contender in this group is indubitably the time-honoured desert ship: the camel. In terms of availability, reliability and economy it has no equal. Comfort and speed are, however, another matter and if you are unfamiliar with the practice of riding camels you should reckon on little of either.

23

To obtain a camel you have only to go to a market town and choose your beast. Most of the larger Saharan towns have markets where camels may be bought; they are often open seven days a week. Prices vary from about £30 to over £1,000. As is usual in life, you get what you pay for—assuming you have only paid the market price. There are two basic varieties of camel. The first is the common or garden 'caravan' camel, brown in colour, with a cruising speed of 3 to 4mph, capable of carrying 250lb of freight and surviving, at a pinch, for 12 days without water. The second is the *Méhari*, or white camel, which will cruise at 6 or 7mph carrying about 180lb for 70 miles a day, but will only survive for around 6 days without water. These camels are highly prized and are not for the beginner. Donkeys or mules are slower, making an average of 20 miles a day. A donkey can only be laden to around 70lb. The chances of making successful purchases without local or professional help are somewhat slender. Since you will presumably also be looking for a guide, it will be best to start this end and make your caravan purchase his first task, having of course established to your satisfaction the credentials of the guide. If you wish for an animal richly caparisoned you will pay a substantial sum— some of the optional extras such as ornate saddles or richly woven bags are decidedly expensive.

Since very few people nowadays make their Saharan exploration by this reliable but slow method, a lengthy treatise on the fitting out of a caravan cannot be justified. But it goes without saying that equipment intended for camels is best purchased locally. Anything you need in the way of personal baggage should be minimal in size and weight. For those who prefer travelling 'heavy' a camel is only practical if you can think of your purchase in the plural. Camels, donkeys, mules and guides may be hired. The latter may cost from £2 to £5 per day and a beast around £1 per day.

Another form of non-automotive transport which has been used for long distance desert crossings is the sand-yacht. A sand-yacht expedition succeeded in travelling from Béchar in north-western Algeria to Nouakchott in Mauretania, following the Moroccan–Algerian and the Spanish Saharan–Mauretanian borders, finishing up along the Mauretanian coast. New sand-yachts cost about £300–£500 and should be so constructed as to be easily repairable. The best time of year for suitable winds combined with moderate temperatures is January when there may be sufficient wind to propel the yachts on three days out of four. Speeds of up to 50mph may be expected on good days. The French are keen on sand-yachting and addresses of sand-yacht builders are given in Appendix D. Sand-yachts should really be considered in conjunction with vehicles: it is not practical to take all you need for long-term survival and yacht repair on such a craft.

Hot air balloons (not obtainable locally) have been used (with support vehicles), as have bicycles. Anyone tough enough to tackle the desert on a bicycle deserves the best and consequently you should equip yourself before departure. So far as I know, no one has yet succeeded in crossing the Sahara on a bicycle. At the time of writing, an Englishman is setting out to cross the Sahara on foot, pulling his baggage behind him on a small trolley.

Automotive transport divides into two distinct groups: cross-country and non cross-country. Much misery and expense has been caused by failing to make this distinction. Certainly it is easy for the distinction to become blurred when reviewing the theoretical capabilities (or at least the claims) of some non cross-country vehicles. To help make this distinction clearer I have gone into the matter much more fully in a separate section on two-wheel versus four-wheel drive vehicles in Chapter 3, but for the moment, let us assume that you will be able to drive all the tarmac roads in your two-wheel drive car. For the other roads and the open desert you will need a four-wheel drive vehicle. So if you want to go in your own vehicle, this is a basic choice that has to be made. If you already have, say, a Land-

Rover, modifications need to be made so, before deciding, read the section on choosing a Land-Rover in Chapter 3. Trailers and caravans are not for the desert.

Turning now to group transport, the most obvious means is to go with one of the companies specialising in Saharan journeys.

A list of organised tour operators will be found in Appendix G. It is not exhaustive. Most of the companies in this field are small, some are undercapitalised and a few lack adequate operating experience. The combination of insufficient money and experience can be unfortunate and there have even been fatalities in the recent past—though not so far as I know with any British operator. I strongly advise would-be patrons to make personal contact with the operators at their place of business, if possible. Much can be judged from such an encounter. These remarks are not intended to form a *caveat* about the small operator—size in itself is no criterion as to the enjoyment you will gain or the safety in which you will travel. Financially, the history of the Saharan tour operation is such that it has not, mercifully, attracted the very large operators. The corollary is that the fares charged are usually very reasonable, and some exploratory costings confirm the point.

What many of these tours have in common is up to eight hours driving a day, sleeping in two-man bivouac tents, tinned food of the cheaper kind, a sharing of chores, forcible feeding by cassette tapes of popular music, and life at close quarters with ten to twenty other people from widely differing backgrounds who may, or may not, share your particular interests. The advantages of this form of Saharan exploration are that, at its best, it can be relatively inexpensive (by utilising low air-charter prices); using air travel to reach the stepping-off point obviously saves time (compared with taking out your own transport). Also, the journey may be planned better than you would have managed, left to your own devices, so that you may see more in the time. There should be no organisational worries and the financial liability should be limited to little more than the cost of the ticket. You may also make new friends and have a great deal of fun. My experience of tour operators has been confined to one such company only, but I have consistently found them especially friendly and helpful.

The disadvantages, all too often apparent, are that you find yourself in a party which is treated like a load of baggage on an express delivery run. If you are unlucky you may find that the expedition leaves perhaps two or three days later than the scheduled date, that the driver never wants to stop for the things that interest you, that little or no interesting background information is provided, that the food is pointlessly repetitive and that the discomforts of group travel are embarrassingly accentuated if you are unfortunate enough to suffer from a severe round of 'gippy tummy'. Itineraries are, on the whole, unimaginative and a tendency is developing for some operators to make a common rat run of certain circuits.

It is important to establish whether you wish to travel with a group of 'young people' (meaning 18 to 35), as several companies specialise in such groups.

Of course, another way of travelling with these companies and being paid to do it is to land yourself a job with one of them as a driver, mechanic or cook. The better ones will give you a pretty thorough going over and will require you to be experienced in driving and maintaining their vehicles.

Finally, there is public transport. You can fly to most of the larger towns and oases in and around the Sahara; it is best to consult a travel agent on availability of flights as the schedules are constantly changing. This is obviously the quickest way of getting into the Sahara but, in my opinion, the least enjoyable. You are unlikely to acquire the 'feel' of the desert which comes if you enter it from its fringes. Schedules are infrequent so you may be stuck for a week—annoying if you happen not to enjoy it.

There are long-distance buses, both scheduled and unscheduled. Scheduled bus services reach most of the towns around the inner fringes and some in the interior. For instance, there is a regular service twice monthly from Ghardaia to Tamanrasset. Unscheduled buses are more often lorries and they leave according to a series of considerations which will not always be comprehensible to the European. In the considerations which are *not* covered may be included the roadworthiness of the vehicle and the adequacy of provisions. They are usually grossly overloaded and extremely uncomfortable. But they represent the best way to travel extensively and cheaply and at the same time to meet and understand the ways of the inhabitants.

The railways are fairly well developed around the fringes. If railway travel is your passion it is best to buy the Michelin Map Number 153 and study the routes. It is a perfectly practical method of reaching such outer-fringe towns as Touggourt or Bamako. For details it is again best to approach a good travel agent who should be able to obtain up-to-date information.

From time to time one sees advertisements in the personal column for passengers to make up a party intending to cross the Sahara or Africa. There is no reason for these not to be genuine but they need to be examined in the light of the advice contained in the relevant sections of this book. It is as well to bear in mind that a lack of pre-departure planning and a careless approach to the whole matter has on occasion ended in complete disaster for those concerned. An African hospital or ail is not everyone's idea of the ideal holiday.

3

Choice of Vehicle

Two-wheel drive vehicles are fine for Saharan exploration, providing you stay on the type of surface for which the vehicle was designed. For most this will almost certainly be tarmac. Tarmac roads in the northern Sahara cover thousands of kilometres. Many of them are of excellent quality and you should have no problem.

The only obvious considerations are spares and repairs; you should find out from the makers of your vehicle the distributive arrangements made in the countries you have decided to visit. Before you go, have the vehicle serviced to the best possible degree; take recommended spares, have new tyres fitted if possible; take as little baggage as you can, but include provision for half a jerrycan of water per passenger and sufficient fuel (including what is in the tank) to give a range of 300 miles. In theory, you will very rarely need this range between petrol stations but, in practice, you may find that intermediate petrol stations are 'temporarily short'. Such shortages sometimes last days.

If you are a mechanic, so much the better, but do not be put off using the more isolated tarmac roads just because you are not. If you do break down you are unlikely to wait more than a few hours, at the most, for a lorry to appear. Its driver will almost certainly mend your engine, or tow you to someone who can. This, though, is where the food and water supplies come in.

It is only when, in spite of all advice to the contrary, you

29

decide to try the *piste* (the non-tarmac tracks) that your problems will almost certainly start. Should the temptation be likely to overcome you, it will be as well to read the section intended for drivers of four-wheel drive vehicles before you leave for the desert.

Have no doubt about it, the allure of the *piste* is very strong. It will probably lead to somewhere which appears especially attractive. The beginning may look extremely easy and you may see a battered and ancient saloon car just emerging. This will probably be a Peugeot, Renault or Citröen of early but indestructable vintage driven by an Arab who knows every inch of the *piste*. In such hands, cars have an altogether different chance of success: with extensive local knowledge these men can avoid the bumps which will break *your* springs (you will see them too late), and by making a detour into the distant desert they will avoid the patches of soft sand in which *you* will stick fast. They do not especially fear breakdown; if they cannot mend the trouble, they are usually better able than Europeans to walk fifty kilometres in a temperature of 100°F toward help if need be and, unlike Europeans, they are never in a hurry.

That people do get hopelessly tempted in this way is, let me hasten to say, quite understandable and as one who has yielded to temptation I must admit that trouble is not *bound* to ensue. It is perhaps the more understandable that saloon cars stray into the province of all-terrain vehicles when one hears, in a general sort of way, of a group of people who 'crossed the Sahara in a Minibus' (usually via the western trans-Saharan *piste*) or when one reads the official advice of the Algerian tourist office in respect of the road, for example, from In Amenas to Djanet. Although departures and arrivals have to be reported, ordinary saloon cars are permitted to circulate on this *piste* individually. There is no reason why one should not emerge at the other end of this *piste*, for example, unscathed; but experience shows that this is seldom the case. It is true that you are fairly unlikely to get stuck for long (though there are many stretches of soft sand) nor are you likely to get lost (though there is one unmarked fork where you might go wrong) but the cumulative effect of the buffetings caused by the corrugated surface are likely to defeat all but the most robust vehicles. Furthermore, the distance from In Amenas to Djanet is 420 miles and, at the time I made this journey, there was no petrol available in Djanet for nineteen days.

I remember vividly the face of a Frenchman I encountered after about a hundred miles. He was driving a new Peugeot—a reasonably strong vehicle—and it was not overladen. He had found that the only way he could get over the corrugations in the surface was to tackle each and every one individually at walking speed: there are some 2,000 corrugations to the mile. He arrived at Djanet several days late, safe but physically exhausted.

I also recall a university teacher and his wife I met at Agadés. They had just arrived from Niamey, a journey which looks on the map just about practicable for a good two-wheel drive vehicle. Theirs was a new small Renault—another vehicle with an excellent rough-going reputation. The car was looking far from new on arrival (several components were missing or broken) but, more significantly, their combined nerve was shattered and when I met them they had just obtained a quotation from an Agadés carrier to put their car on a lorry and deliver it to Tamanrasset—not very far and a regular lorry route; they, however, were asked £250 for the service.

These were people who, nevertheless, got through successfully. Indeed, it is perfectly possible especially on the most westerly of the two trans-Sahara routes but, in my view, it would be irresponsible to recommend it to the inexperienced. I have met many who did not get through and seen the wrecked cars of many more; a sad and often expensive end to what promised to be a great adventure. It is wiser to decide before leaving whether or not you intend to hazard your vehicle as well as subject yourself and your passengers to the possibility of a long drawn out, uncomfortable and expensive recovery operation.

If you do decide not to risk it, you can be sure of one thing: the very next saloon car you meet, which will be an older and a less suitable car than yours, driven by simpletons without provisions or spares, will have just completed the very *piste* you wanted to do—without the slightest difficulty! Similarly, if you obtain a Land-Rover and fit it out in accordance with the advice given, you can be sure that as you peer beneath the bonnet in search of some elusive fault you will be overtaken by a group of students in an ancient Land-Rover totally un-modified and purchased in a farm sale, untried, for £50.

Two-wheel drive vehicles

Of the two-wheel drive vehicles that attempt the *piste*, the most common and perhaps the best is the Volkswagen Minibus. Nonetheless, the abandoned, and often burnt out, wrecks of these vehicles are also the most numerous. Many do survive, overladen though they frequently are, no doubt partly due to the good basic design of the vehicle and partly to the list of all recommended modifications, spares and tools which Volks-wagen issue (in English) for the operation of their vehicles under such conditions. See Appendix D for Volkswagen's address.

The smallest size of Citröen—particularly the old 2cv— Renault and Peugeot, as well as the ubiquitous Volkswagen beetle, are all strong contenders. In general, French cars are well understood in the Saharan countries and second-hand spare parts are often obtainable in remote places.

Ground clearance is important; if you are proceeding south through central Africa you will need to be able to cope with the nine-inch central ridge of Congo tracks.

The single greatest cause of failure is overloading. It is all very well to say 'I will not overload.' When you are faced with the demands of, say, the relatively simple journey to Tamanrasset, you will have to pile into your vehicle not only your own camping and personal gear but a considerable weight of spares, food and water and enough petrol for 600 miles. It is, of course, tempting to include two extra passengers to help share the costs. Even before the journey is attempted the springs will not be looking too happy.

There are modifications which can be carried out to saloon cars, such as strengthening the springs, but mostly such work is of an *ad hoc* nature. Conversions of this type tend to reduce the value of saloon cars because they admit to the vehicle having had a terrible bashing, whereas a similar conversion to a Land-Rover—however paradoxically—actually increases its value.

Self-drive saloon cars are generally available throughout the Saharan countries. Hiring is likely to be more expensive than taking your own—unless you plan a very short journey—and you face the additional problem of transporting your baggage all the way to the starting point. In Algeria, for instance, there are at least twenty towns in which you can hire cars. To hire an average saloon and make a circuit of 2,000 miles during two weeks might easily cost you £150. To find out exact prices write to the Tourist Office, or its equivalent, of each country (see Appendix D), stating the name of the town from which you wish to start, the period of hire and which other countries you wish to visit. The principle of 'hire it here, leave it there' is not generally accepted in Saharan countries.

To hire a Volkswagen Minibus in England will cost about £70 per week, unlimited mileage.

Four-wheel drive vehicles

It should be plain from earlier remarks that the Saharan *piste* really demands four-wheel drive vehicles. The theoretical choice is wide, the practical choice is not.

However much you may favour this or that make, you will have to consider available spares and technically skilled service. For reasons that will be made more apparent in the section on spares later in this chapter, it is not feasible to carry every spare you might need. As you could easily be stuck for weeks or even months if the piece has to be sent from America or Japan you are, at this particular moment and whether you like it or not, forced to conclude that the best type of vehicle for the purpose is the Land-Rover. With time and increasing foreign competition—particularly Japanese—this situation may change but it will not happen quickly.

There are many small four-wheel drive vehicles available, some of which are both well made and cheap to buy, possibly because they are obsolete, and occasionally one comes across them, often abandoned. Amongst the better known are the Jeep, Dodge Power Wagon, Austin Gypsy and Haflinger. In a different category—because both are the subject of a powerful sales drive—are the Toyota and the Range Rover. In their present form and without the wide availability of spares and technical know-how, neither in my view is worth considering.

The Land-Rover owes its absolute supremacy to the fact that it is a highly successful vehicle in its own right, endlessly proven under desert conditions, with a spare parts availability and a technical expertise (largely unofficial) resulting from its having been a market leader for a quarter of a century: official estimates are that 45,000 Land-Rovers have been sold to Saharan countries. Quite simply there is no other vehicle that comes even remotely into this category. This is not to say that other vehicles are not good or that they are certain to need spares and repairs, but due to the nature of Saharan travel, the chances that they will need attention are high and the chances of your being greatly inconvenienced equally high.

It is said that in the Sahara there are three basic units of currency—the currency of the individual countries, Maria-Theresa sovereigns and Land-Rover spare parts. I can certainly confirm the validity of the last. Such is the demand that I have seen serviceable second, third or fourteenth-hand components change hands for double their UK market price. A glance at the

Page 35
SAHARAN SCENERY
5 The volcanic peaks of the Hoggar mountains—the summits are some 8,000–9,000ft high; a good *piste* may be seen in the valley
6 The comparatively lush vegetation of the Aïr mountains; area such as these are full of wildlife

SAHARAN
SCENERY
7 Tarmac road
over the
Moroccan Atlas,
one of the main
approaches to
the north-
western Sahara
8 Near Fort
Gardel in the
Tassili region

illustration on page 90 showing vehicles queueing for petrol at an oasis emphasises the general popularity of this vehicle.

You will see relatively few garages of the type one associates with repair facilities. But this is no indication at all that the mud-brick house beside you does not contain a mechanical genius, nor that the *pisé* wall surrounding his yard is not full of Land-Rover spare parts.

Alas, there is no list published of the actual facilities available to Land-Rover owners. It would be far more useful than the official list of agents and distributors; officially there is no Land-Rover agent in Agadés on the trans-Saharan *piste*. In fact there are several and repair facilities in this neat mud-built town, though hidden from the passer-by, extend to a total rebuild or to the precision machining of engine components. I have, for example, witnessed Mr Bashir Sadek of that town demonstrate a remarkable Land-Rover expertise in assembling faultlessly the numerous components which form the front axle assembly, in the pitch dark, on a Sunday! Where in Britain would you find such a singular talent?

New is not always *best*. Specifications tend to become more economical; pointless styling costs more money; new design modifications often made to meet the demands of foreign markets may not be fully proven and parts not widely available.

A word should be added about four-wheel drive lorries, such as the Bedford Truck (no longer in production), the Mercedes Unimog (chassis with platform body only of model S is about £4,500 delivered UK) or the six-wheel drive Studebaker Rio Truck (which seems to get stuck as much as a four-wheel drive truck). All are good theoretical contenders. From the point of view of economy and spares I recommend the Bedford—it can be made to seat twenty or so—and if nothing serious goes wrong it can provide the cheapest *per capita* cost of a Saharan journey.

For all the reasons given in this chapter, I chose a nine-year old Land-Rover Series IIA model with its first 100,000 miles just appearing on the clock.

Choosing a Land-Rover

If you have been persuaded that a suitable vehicle in which to cruise the Sahara is, in fact, a Land-Rover, you will need to choose a particular model from amongst the numerous types available.

Long or short wheelbase? Hard or soft top? New or second hand? Petrol or diesel?

As mentioned, *new* is not always *best*. Land-Rovers are best seen as combinations of interchangeable components which can be built up as required. This means that you can save yourself the expense of a new vehicle as well as a lengthy and possibly interminable hunt for 'just the specification'. There are a number of ingeniously devised (and usually expensive) standard conversions available, but built-in stoves, sinks and cupboards are a nuisance and quite impractical.

Apart from the high cost of a new Series III Land-Rover (about £2,600 suitably adapted) the earlier Series IIA is far more widely distributed in the desert. Most Saharan Land-Rover drivers seem to consider that the Series IIA specification was, in any case, more suited to the purpose than the plusher Series III, although the Series III is bound to become better known and, of course, much of the gadgetry can be removed. For the time being, though, a Series IIA is likely to be the happier choice—it is again the ever-present factor of spares.

There are two basic types, the short wheelbase (88in) and the long (109in). Arguments as to which is the more suitable have raged ever since the two types became available. Purists prefer the short wheelbase; they assume—as purists do—that you are going to travel light, and base their preference on adequate carrying capacity, slightly better performance, improved manoeuvrability and clearance and slightly lower price.

As the argument seems interminable I will only say that almost all the expedition Land-Rovers you will encounter in the Sahara—as opposed to the car park of the local public house in England—will be long wheelbase. The fact is that theoretical niceties of performance, manoeuvrability and clearance count for little in the desert: the long wheelbase works perfectly adequately. Whether you use the capacity or not, you will never regret having it. There may be times—during a sand storm for instance—when it is useful to be able to move around inside. If everything is piled up to the roof it is not only time consuming and irritating to extricate the thing you want, but it is harder to secure the load and you sacrifice backward visibility; and on certain types of corrugated surface the shorter wheelbase gives a substantially rougher ride.

Hard or soft top—in other words, a metal or canvas roof behind the cab? Unquestionably, hard top! A writer should avoid being didactic; but if my purpose is to save others making mistakes, what is the point of pulling the punches? A canvas top is a joke! You will seldom see them but, when you do, prepare to be amused at someone else's expense. The last one I saw transported an English farmer and his wife who had just completed the crossing of a hot desert made up of particles of the finest red dust. Inside the vehicle, baggage and passengers were a uniform red. It seemed somehow strange to see these sand sculptures actually moving and talking!

Petrol or diesel? The advantages of the petrol engine are a higher power and torque output, a higher maximum speed, quietness of operation, it is generally more easily understood than a diesel, a petrol Land-Rover is less expensive to purchase, petrol is a cleaner and less pungent fuel. The advantages of the diesel engine are the absence of an ignition system (a great help in negotiating water and where there is a fire risk), lower fuelling costs, considerably lower fuel consumption and diesel fuel is more readily available than petrol in some parts of the world. Simply because it is more generally understood, I would recommend the petrol engine, though this consideration is not of fundamental importance.

A suitably modified Series IIA Land-Rover in good 'expedition' repair could cost £1,400–£1,800.

Specification and modification

The basic specification is, therefore, long wheelbase, hard top and, for the time being, Series IIA.

You must now consider the following modifications which are all, in my opinion, to be highly recommended:

1 ton rear springs and shackles
Heavy duty front springs and shackles
Heavy duty (Range-Rover) rear axle and differential
Heavy duty (reinforced) front axle
Heavy duty shock absorbers, front and rear
Protection shield of ¼in steel plate bolted to chassis beneath gear box.

Jerrycan carriers for 2 cans in front of front wings (see note on jerrycans, page 61).

Jerrycan carriers for 3 cans either side of vehicle above rear wheels.

Roof-rack of maximum length including provision for 8 jerrycans. My personal recommendation is to utilise this space in the manner illustrated on plates 14 and 18. The canvas top (which is a standard soft-top canvas roof with an additional end-flap sown in) contains sleeping quarters. This area is fitted with a foam (or plastic) mattress 78in × 56in and provides a permanent, comfortable 'tent' without the inconvenience of a collapsible tent which has to be pitched each night. If the flaps are kept shut, very little dust enters at this height. There is also space for sleeping bags and other bulky but light things and you are out of the reach of many insects, scorpions, and all but the most ingenious snakes. When the nights are warm, the canvas can be rolled back. The roof-rack also contains space for a large tin trunk, supplies of oil, distilled water, a stack of firewood and, as mentioned, 8 jerrycans.

Front winch; there are two types, a drum winch with a 4,000lb pull and a capstan with a 2,500lb pull. The advantage of the drum winch is that it is more powerful and more convenient, since the steel hawser is wound on the drum ready for use, and it can be operated solely by the driver from the safety of his cab.

The advantage of the capstan is that it is cheaper and lighter. The disadvantage of both is that they are expensive and weigh you down. My recommendation is that one vehicle in a party should have one or other winch. If you are travelling solo, you should have a capstan winch. However, a winch of any kind is definitely a luxury.

Special Air Filter

Towing points (for towing and being towed) front and rear.

Rear flap and platform (as opposed to rear door). This gives a useful out-of-the-rain working surface.

Window protection; for any non-opening windows which are only retained by means of a rubber channel it is worth considering a continuous band of pig-wire (or similar wire mesh) welded to the inside. It not only provides security but saves window damage from things getting thrown around inside. It also serves as an invaluable anchor for the baggage retaining 'spiders'.

Locks for spare wheels, jerrycans, fuel cap, bonnet and doors—better and cheaper than insurance.

Deluxe seat for driver. It is much more comfortable for driving and holds you more securely than the standard bench seat. It is not a good idea to have a similar passenger seat since it is more convenient and comfortable for the passenger to have greater freedom of movement.

Interior strip light of the low consumption fluorescent type.

Fire extinguishers; it is best to have one below driver's seat and another on the tail flap.

Boomerang external mirrors or extensions to provide vision past side of the jerrycan racks.

Front and rear reflectors on jerrycan racks.

Extended axle check straps

Flyscreens for dash vents.

Reversing lamp with a wide spread.

Seat belts

Sun visors only if you do not have the recommended roof-rack.

Wire mesh guard on front lights.

Additional headlights mounted on front of roof-rack. Only necessary if you intend to do much night travelling on the way to Africa; travelling the desert at night is a dangerous practice.

Battery; a new one if possible.

Extra fuel tanks; a 10 gallon tank beneath the passenger seat saves the need to carry 2 jerrycans and improves the centre of gravity. An exterior filling arrangement should be provided to avoid fuel being spilled inside the vehicle.

Heater; apart from being a generally valuable fitting, this will be most welcome during the journey both for heating the vehicle and cooling the engine.

Hand throttle; a convenience for long distances.

Spare wheel carrier on bonnet and roof-rack; do not fit to rear door.

Tropical roof should be fitted only if roof-rack is not fitted.

Windscreen pillars may need reinforcement on Series III Land-Rovers if roof-rack is fitted. Check also bonnet hinges and clamps.

Strong-box may be welded on to provide added security for money and valuables.

Vice; this is a useful fitting on front bumber.

Engine temperature gauge, if not already fitted, is useful.

8-bladed fan (part number 605553 for Series IIA Land-Rover).

Exhaust manifold; due to problems of corrosion it is a good plan to remove existing studs and replace with stainless steel studs and brass nuts. A manifold gasket should be fitted.

Hydraulic steering damper to cushion the vibrations.

Alternative carburettor jets are available for prolonged use above 5,000, 7,000, 9,000 and 12,000 feet respectively but, although you may spend some time above 5,000 feet, it is not a necessary modification.

Tyres deserve a special mention; on these depend your security. To have three punctures in the open desert (assuming you have two spare wheels but no spare tubes) is a disaster. Worn or unsuitable tyres are a major risk—Saharan terrain will quickly find out which tyres are worth having. If possible, start with a new set for although expensive in England they are prohibitive in the Sahara. Even though you may not need them, it is worth taking two spare wheels, rather than spare covers; the fitting of covers to wheels under conditions of great heat is a game to be avoided. If you are intending to cruise on sand only, the best tyre is the Michelin XS, and if on rough terrain and sand (which is far more likely) the Michelin XY is my very strong recommendation. It is suggested that inner tubes are fitted.

Other 'extras' which may not be desirable for one reason or another are swivel housing gaiters, oil coolers (except with 6-cylinder models operating in a very high ambient temperature), free-wheeling hubs, burglar alarms and outside steps.

Trailers under conditions of soft sand are a failure; they are often the straw which breaks the mechanical camel's back. They can cause you to become stuck and prevent you becoming unstuck.

Fitting-out the Land-Rover

It is likely that you will want to have all, or most, of this major fitting work carried out by a garage experienced in the specialised work of conversion, even though this may not be the garage from which you purchased the vehicle.

My own Land-Rover supply and conversion was carried out by Brian Bashall of Dunsfold Land-Rovers, Dunsfold, Surrey whose enthusiasm and resourcefulness in carrying out expedition modification is difficult to match. He also has the distinction of being the 'inventor' of the soft-top on hard-top double-decker arrangement.

Land-Rover hire

Hiring Land-Rovers for expedition purposes is unlikely to be economical, either in this country or abroad, but it can be done. See Appendix E for addresses. Prices may be in the order of

£225 per month (unlimited mileage) for a vehicle which may not be appropriately modified.

In the Sahara you may, or may not, find a suitable vehicle for hire—it is best to approach the matter through the local tourist offices. However, for a month's cruise of 2,000 miles the figure—again for a vehicle which may not be suitably modified —may be at least £400.

Tools

The Rover Company suggests carrying the tools listed in Appendix F on expeditions and many of these are issued with a new vehicle. I have also listed some additional items which may be useful.

Oil; good quality oil is not always available and the price is always high. You may suffer an oil leak. For these reasons you should leave Europe with sufficient oil for a complete oil change.

Spares; another subject on which the veterans disagree. The main considerations are these: the more you take, the heavier the load, and the greater the chance of component failure; there is reduced value in including anything which you yourself cannot fit and the selection must be adapted to the age and condition of the vehicle (it is therefore difficult to provide a definitive list for used vehicles); an exceptionally large inventory may attract the expensive attention of customs officers; several vehicles travelling together means fewer spares need be carried all round.

For my own Series IIA LWB Land-Rover, the Rover Company suggested for a Saharan journey spares to a UK retail value of £86. In the course of the journey in question I needed spares to an approximate UK value of £60. None of the spares I needed was on the Rover list. But I do not regard this as their fault; they did not inspect the vehicle before making the list and amongst the spares I needed was a complete axle housing, which it would have been quite impractical to take.

My alternative approach to the matter of relevant spares has been to consult someone who has had extensive experience of driving and maintaining Land-Rovers under desert conditions. The list in Appendix F was made by Mr Jim Page who has such experience. It has been compiled for LWB Series III Petrol engine Land-Rovers engaging on a major expedition of up to 20,000 miles. Of course, many of the components will be applicable to Series II vehicles.

Maintenance

However unmechanical he may be, the owner or driver *must* learn to perform routine maintenance. It is very simple on a Land-Rover, the more so as it can be achieved without the necessity of jacking the vehicle up as there is sufficient clearance to lie beneath, though this is made the easier if the vehicle is parked astride a small depression or ditch.

For the more mechanically ambitious or the more security-minded, there is no substitute to working in a Land-Rover garage for some time. The Rover Company run three-day Land-Rover maintenance courses from time to time. It is advisable to book well in advance. Details of these can be obtained from the Service School at Solihull; see Appendix D for address. Very obviously the inconvenience, delay and expense you will incur is likely to be directly proportional to your mechanical aptitude. A list of used Land-Rover dealers is to be found in Appendix E.

4

Planning a Cruise

Almost everyone makes the mistake of overcrowding their itinerary when planning their journey.

The distance that can be comfortably achieved will depend on such a variety of factors that it is impossible to suggest more than the vaguest guidelines. For the tarred roads of the northern desert anything up to 300 miles a day is perfectly feasible, though there are many interesting places to visit in certain areas and a figure of 150 might be a more intelligent target. Over the major and well maintained *pistes* and over flat, hard desert a good 200 miles can be covered without strain but again this leaves little or no time for sight-seeing.

For the rest it is almost meaningless to give a figure; it could vary from 30 (or even less) to 150 miles or so a day. Since at the planning stage you are unlikely to know the condition of all the roads, there is nothing for it but to calculate progress by means of a general average. 100 miles a day is a comfortable figure, 150 is a good average, while 200 is definitely on the steep side. These figures include a good share of tarmac distances, such as the outward journey from Britain. Do not be tempted into large daily averages; you will be exhausted and miss a great deal of interest. However, in emergency one can achieve higher figures—I have driven the 3,000 miles from Agadés to Britain in 10 days but it took another 10 days to recover.

Costs

Apart from ferries, the major expense will be in fuel. You will

46

no doubt know the fuel consumption figures for your vehicle, but as soon as you are in the desert these figures will fall. In the case of a heavily laden long wheelbase Land-Rover, giving 16mpg on tarmac, you will probably only average about 11mpg over long desert crossings. Therefore for such a vehicle the average might be around 13mpg and a journey of 5,000 miles will thus take some 385 gallons.

Fuel prices vary according to the country or even the region. For instance, in Algeria prices are controlled and tourist subsidies available, so that petrol may be bought in limited quantities for about 25p a gallon. You can also obtain fuel coupons, at low rates, for Morocco. Apply to the Standard Bank of West Africa with passport and car log book. In the far-flung oasis of Bilma, in the Niger, it may be four times this price. On a recent trans-Saharan journey, petrol cost an average of 40p per gallon. Some people drive across the Sahara planning to ship their vehicle back from a West African port such as Lagos. It is not a simple operation and it is also extremely expensive—around £300.

Ferries can easily account for another £30–£200, not including passenger tickets which might each be £25 plus.

The cost of special equipment and camping gear will depend entirely on the ambitions of the expedition and whether it can be borrowed—it usually can. Vehicle modifications, if applicable, must be calculated separately according to the extent of the work required. Similarly spares and tools.

Food costs a considerable amount but it is probably reasonable to regard it as being free since a roughly similar expenditure would have been incurred at home. Medicines, first-aid kit, maps, special clothes and other items may not exceed £50.

Insurance is the only other significant item and it can be considerable. Apart from third party cover (which has to be purchased separately in Algeria and, on occasion, in Morocco) it is as well to consider if it really is worth the premium. If the vehicle has been made secure it is not, in my opinion, worth insuring the contents, with the exception perhaps of cameras or binoculars. Neither do I feel it is worth insuring against breakdown. Cover is, in any case, either difficult or impossible to arrange. But medical expenses are, I think, well worth covering and should include the cost of being flown back in an emergency. While essential vehicle insurances may cost as little as £20, full cover against all the possible risks might cost a premium of £200. For personal insurance providing £1,000 for medical expenses, £1,000 for partial, permanent disablement or death, £300 for baggage loss and £100,000 for personal liability, the premium can be as low as £3–£4 per person for a two-week period. Cancellation insurance is also worth considering where non-refundable fares have been paid. The Norwich Union specialises in cover of this category.

Other costs likely to be encountered on the journey are probably confined to breakdowns, additional food, tips, souvenirs and oil for the vehicle. Except for breakdowns, £50 per head should be more than adequate unless the expedition is intended to be very long. I suppose it is impossible to have too much money in the event of breakdowns (or illness) but a reasonable figure might be £200 (for the vehicle) and £100 reserve for contingencies for each passenger. Bank credit cards are very little practical use and the Automobile Association's 5-Star service credit vouchers supposed to be valid in all Saharan countries except Chad, Libya, Mali, Mauretania, Niger and the Spanish Sahara are, in my experience, about as useful as a sheet of blank paper!

To summarise—leaving aside vehicle costs and/or modification, spares, tools, depreciation—the actual costs associated with a 5,000 miles cruise for four people in a Land-Rover might be in the order of £700, allowing something for mishaps. Making allowance for these omissions, the figure might be more like £1,200, or £300 per head, which compares not unfavourably with the fare charged by a tour operator—though a comparison of costs is of course only one of the considerations.

Passengers

It is very tempting, for reasons of work-sharing and economy, to 'sell' all the passenger seats you have. This is a great mistake since each passenger increases the likelihood of failure through overloading. You also reduce the storage room and your capacity to accommodate such desirable extras as a second spare wheel.

Again, everything will depend on your chosen route. If it is on tarmac and you are staying in hotels, there is no reason why the vehicle should not be fully occupied. But if you are doing long-range desert crossings the ideal number is unquestionably a driver and one passenger only. If you are driving a Land-Rover and are three, it is much better (and safer) to put the second passenger behind the front seats; the jump seat in the centre is quite impractical for long journeys.

Weight and space

Early on during the preparations it is a good idea to make a baggage calculation. This should be done both for cubic content and weight. Due allowance in both respects should be made for passengers, water (10lb a gallon) and petrol (9lb a gallon). The results of this calculation are usually alarming but it is no good ignoring them!

Passports and currency regulations

Allow sufficient time to obtain the visas you need (see Appendix C); remember that if travelling with your wife you need only one passport and this can save several pounds on visas. Take ten spare passport photographs. Your passport must not bear stamps or visas connected with Israel, South Africa, Rhodesia or Portuguese territories. Ask your bank for a copy of the Bank of England's *Notice to Travellers*; it will give you current information on currency allowances, exchange control restrictions, use of bank cards and other fiscal information.

International Driving Permits and Carnet de Passages en Douane

Contact the Automobile Association. You must have a full current UK licence and be over eighteen years old.

General

After the route has been selected, and the number of passengers determined, the following list may be helpful as a basic check-list.

Vehicle: purchase or adapt—thoroughly check and test—obtain maintenance training if required—tools (see Appendix F)—spares (see Appendix F)—fuel and water calculations—customs' Carnet—insurance and Green Card—ferry reservations.

Passengers: passports—visas—inoculations (see Appendix C)—clothes (see Chapter 9)—international driving licence—insurance—currency and travellers cheques—ferry reservations.

Equipment: camping gear (see Chapter 8)—food (see Chapter 10)—medicines and first-aid kit (see Chapter 15)—maps (see Chapter 7)—miscellanea (see Chapters 6 and 9)—insurance.

5

Where, When and How

There is so much that is personal in Saharan exploration that no two people will value the same place equally. So, in the limited space I can do no more than touch on some of the main areas which attract a majority of people. Although many regions are justly famous, it is the subjective element in desert travel which will probably exert the strongest influence. Put another way, by all means plan to visit one of the 'sights' but do not in the least discount the other areas through which you pass. The map overleaf locates the regions listed.

A *Middle and Southern Morocco*

The fabulous city of Marrakesh is an excellent starting point for excursions over the High Atlas into the desert's northern fringes. A journey down the Dra valley to M'hamid on the disputed Moroccan–Algerian frontier or a journey eastward from Ouarzazate to Tinerhir and the Gorge of Todra is full of interest with spectacular scenery and extraordinarily attractive mud forts (*ksars* and *kasbas*). Further east still, there are the numerous oases of the valley of the Ziz leading south to Erfoud where there is a campsite.

B *The Tanezrouft and Western Desert*

The largest area of uninterrupted desert in the Sahara; its main appeal is to those with experience wishing to mount a major expedition. Nonetheless, the Western trans-Saharan

51

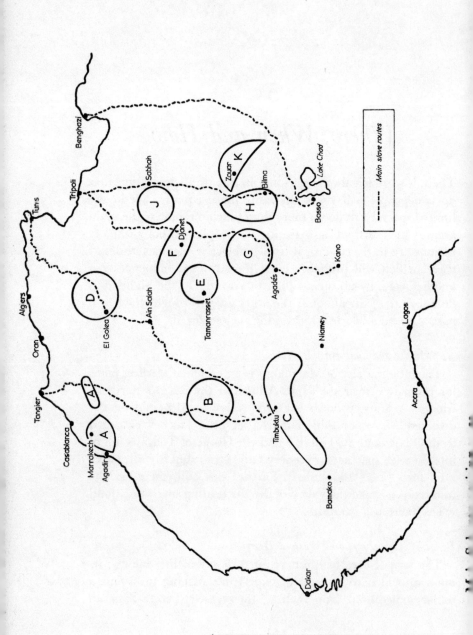

Main slave routes

Benghazi

Tripoli

Tunis

Algiers

Oran

Tangier

Casablanca

Marrakech

Agadir

A'

A

D

El Golea

Ain Salah

B

Tamanrasset

E

F

Djanet

J

Sabhah

K

Zouar

H

Bilma

Bosso

Lake Chad

G

Agadés

Kano

Niamey

Timbuktu

C

Bamako

Dakar

Accra

Lagos

Page 53 SAHARAN SCENERY
9 Ravine near In Guezzam, Southern Algeria
10 A *pise* casbah in the Dra Valley, Morocco. Such mud-built villages frequently boast an astonishing wealth of architectural detail and surface ornamentation

Page 54 TYPES OF SURFACE

11 A typical section of hard *piste* on the Fadnoun plateau—the characteristic dust cloud is more visible than the vehicle itself. A mild example of washboard surface is to be seen in the foreground

12 Hard sand and gravel, usually easy. Scrub-covered surfaces are often good but it is important to avoid the tufts

motor route (Reggane, Bidon 5, Gao) passes through the edge
of this desert. This trans-Saharan *piste* is the easier of the two
and leads towards the interesting area of the Upper Niger.

C   Upper Niger
Interesting towns along the Niger, the Dogon country (home
of West African troglodytes), the vanished glories of Timbuktu
and the spectacular river scenes of Gao. The whole area is rich
with wild life.

D   Northern Algerian oases
The oases of Ghardaia, Touggourt, Ouargla and El Goléa
are all easy of access on hard-surfaced roads from Algiers or
Tunis. These oases contain much of interest and the road between them passes through a flattish desert sandwiched between
two great seas of sand dunes, the Great Eastern Erg and the
Great Western Erg.

E   The Hoggar Massif
Perhaps the best known area in the Sahara. Easily accessible
by the Eastern trans-Saharan *piste* (which is shortly due to be
tarmac-surfaced all the way to Tamanrasset—at present it
reaches to Ain Salah) it is the western part of the Massif that
is best known. Impressive volcanic 'plugs' soar 10,000 feet into
the sky. Principal pilgrimage is to the hermitage of Father
Foucauld (at 9,000ft) from which the panorama is un-
forgettable. Capital of the region is the mountain oasis of
Tamanrasset, exploited by the Algerian government for tourist
and mining purposes but dying from water shortage and active
resentment on the part of the native.

F   The Tassili n'Ajjer plateau
This is the eastern part of the Hoggar Massif. It consists of an
extraordinary 'lunar' landscape of total desolation. The
crumbling mountains have eroded into fantastic, often colum-

D

nar, shapes. The area has been called the open-air museum of pre-historic art on account of the thousands of rock paintings and other prehistoric traces spread over dozens of sites, many still virtually inaccessible. Djanet oasis is the centre for this region.

G *The Aïr Mountains*

Normally reached from Agadés, this huge mountainous terrain is little known. The scenery of the Aïr is rugged and attractive and there is an abundant wild life, especially in its variety of birds; some of the valleys are well wooded. This is an area of particular interest to archaeologists.

H *The Ténéré Desert*

One of the most formidable sand barriers in the Sahara. Partly a vast expanse of flat sand and partly a sea of sand dunes, its crossing is still a formidable undertaking. Sand storms are not uncommon. If approached from Agadés the crossing is usually made to the salt producing oasis of Bilma, otherwise directly to Djanet.

I *The Libyan Fezzan*

The road from Tripoli, via Sebhah toward Ghat and Djanet passes between two sand seas. This valley is another prehistoric art gallery which can be approached on a hard-surfaced road as far as Awbari.

J *The Tibesti Mountains*

One of the most inaccessible areas of the Sahara. The massif of the Tibesti contains several extremely high peaks, the tallest being the volcanic cone of Emi Koussi, 11,200ft. This enormous area has very few tracks but there are interesting oases, rock paintings, tombs, hot springs, gorges, weird geological formations, baboons, vultures and naked men. The 'easiest' approach is from Largeau in Chad.

When to go

In general, the months of May to September are considered too hot for Saharan exploration. In mid-summer the heat can be appalling and hot winds and dust storms can add to the discomfort. In the southern Sahara especially, mid-summer is the time of the rains and often the *pistes* are impassable. This applies to both the trans-Saharan routes. If you are crossing the Sahara *en route* for equatorial Africa, you will also need to avoid the rains there which extend more or less across the summer months. December to February are probably the best months for the deep Sahara. Spring and autumn are less predictable than the winter months but otherwise satisfactory.

How to get there

It is impossible to give much advice on the subject as the choice must depend on financial considerations, time available, type of vehicle as well as sight-seeing *en route*.

The quickest way could be to send the vehicle by train to Marseilles and take the ferry to Algiers. However, most expedition vehicles, by the time they are fitted out with roof-racks, side-racks for jerrycans and so on, exceed the maximum dimensions permitted on French railways. The journey involving the least trouble is perhaps the car ferry *Eagle* from Southampton to Tangier. The cheapest way is no doubt to drive to Algeciras and take the short ferry crossing to Ceuta.

However, the permutations are legion. There are vehicle-carrying ferries from Marseilles to Oran, Algiers, Skikda and Annaba; from Genoa and Naples to Tunis and Tripoli. Trans-Mediterranean ferries leave, in my opinion, a good bit to be desired in the matter of comfort and service and this particularly applies to the ferries from Marseilles, some of which are without cabins. A single crossing for a laden Land-Rover (without passengers) is likely to cost you around £80 Marseilles/Algiers, French Line or £50 Genoa/Tunis, Italian General Shipping Limited (see Appendix D for addresses).

6

Equipment

For ease of reference I have listed below, in alphabetical order, an assortment of gear, some or all of which you may need, or think of taking, together with explanatory notes:

Bags, insulated — Good for keeping food cool. Provided you put in enough first thing in the morning, food stays surprisingly cold for several hours.

Bags, polythene — A good assortment is essential. They keep bread, fruit and vegetables fresh; useful for laundry (whether clean or dirty) and many other things. Take a selection of sizes from about 12in × 8in to 24in × 12in and also at least one large strong fertiliser-type bag (see page 78).

Bottle — Personal, for water, while on the move. Some have a canvas exterior which, if wetted, helps to cool water.

Bottles, plastic — Keep one full of water in a very handy place for burns. A spare one is always useful. Large collapsible ones might be more useful if they did not chafe and puncture so easily.

Bowl, washing — My preference is for the canvas type that sits on the top of a folding stand. Due to the cooling effect of evaporation from the wet canvas this will also double as a method of cooling beer. A canvas bath is a great luxury.

Bowl, washing up   Plastic, and not too small.

Boxes, plastic   Several small ones for food and one 8in × 8in × 3½in for untinned cake.

Brush   A soft one for sweeping sand from vehicle.

Bucket, polythene   You will find various uses but its prime function is to extract water from wells. For this purpose the best type is the collapsible 'inner tube' bucket, for some wells are extremely shallow.

Camera   Take all the films you think you will need. It is cheaper and safer. (See note on cameras and films at end of chapter.)

Chopping/ Bread board

Cigarettes   Unless you smoke yourself it is better to purchase locally if they are intended as gifts. In many countries they are far cheaper than in Britain.

Cleaner   A hand cleaner such as Swarfega for removing ingrained oil and grease.

Clothes pegs   At least 6 per head.

Compass   See section on *pistes* and open desert (Chapter 11).

Contraband   It is extremely foolish to presume that you will not be caught or that, if you are, you will not suffer a severe punishment.

Cooking utensils   Knives, wooden spoons, measure, sieve, grater, mixing bowl.

Cooking stove   See note on this at end of chapter.

Cook's table   Folding or camp kitchen. Particularly useful because of the shelter it provides for the stove. Some fold flat and others incorporate a large space for accessories. It is important to have a lightweight one.

Cord	100ft nylon for drawing bucket from well, plus a further 100ft spare.
Corks	A few may come in handy.
Corkscrew	If not on pocket knife.
Cushions	One or two small ones can be a great improvement to comfort.
Cutlery	One seldom takes too much. Stainless steel is the most practical.
Distress flare	If you are leaving the *piste*, orange and black flares.
Elastic bands	A few, if strong and unperished.
Enamel mugs	With handle, for hot soup.
Field glasses	Not much use for horizontal observation, due to mirage and shimmering effect of hot desert. But invaluable for observation of birds or mountain scenery.
Firearms	Do not take these. They are quite unnecessary and you will have trouble with the frontier officials.
Flower press	If flowers interest you this is indispensable because in desert heat picked flowers can be unrecognisable within a few hours.
Flywhisk	As good as anything else for dealing with flies and produces fanning effect as well.
Foil	For cooking purposes. Also useful as a food wrap.
Funnels, metal with gauze	
	One small one for filling petrol or paraffin stoves and one large one for filling vehicle with fuel (not needed on Land-Rover).
Funnels, plastic	One large one for filling jerrycans from a water bucket.
Gauze, metal	For spreading and lowering heat from stove.
Gloves, rubber	For washing up.
Goggles	For sand storms. A useful aid. Some people

	prefer them to dark glasses for ordinary use but they are hot to wear.
Jerrycans, for water	Thick-gauge plastic ones; ex-army are best. 6 for major expeditions.
Jug	For water.
Kettle	The enclosed type is best; or 'Volcano' type.
Mallet	For tent pegs and recalcitrant objects.
Matches	Safety variety only and double the quantity you think you will need.
Orange squeezer	For use when encountering a glut of low-priced oranges.
Paper, rolls of	General purpose kitchen type (absorbent) invaluable for washing up, drying, removing sand, drying hands and so on. A large roll a week per vehicle.
Paper, toilet	50 per cent more than your calculations indicate!
Pocket knife	Use varies according to range of blades provided.
Presents	A good supply will prove invaluable. Safe bets for children everywhere are sugar lumps, boiled sweets, pens, pencils and exercise books. Presents for adults will depend on locality and the status of the individual concerned and, of course, the value of the service, if any, rendered. Presents are, however, usually better than money. Cigarettes are almost always acceptable but the niceties of expensive brands rather wasted. Whisky in Algeria, where it is some £12 a bottle, hardly ever fails even among technically teetotal Moslems. Tea and coffee can be useful as gifts but it is as well to remember that tea of the very highest quality is widely

	obtainable in the Sahara and coffee is not drunk much by the desert Arab.
Pressure cooker	Saves fuel and water.
Pricker, for stove	If you have a pressure stove without a built-in self-pricking device one or two of these are indispensable.
Refrigerator	Too heavy and unreliable under desert conditions. The new type gas/electric 'caravan' refrigerators are fine if you stick to the tarmac.
Sand ladders	Take 2 (see Chapter 11).
Saucepans	At least 2, preferably 3. Size according to number in party but graded so that they fit inside each other. All should have lids, both to facilitate rapid heating and to prevent sand getting into food while cooking. Polaris stainless steel are to be recommended.
Scourer	Useful aid for washing cookpots.
Sheet	Large canvas or plastic (12ft × 9ft or larger) to form awning from side of vehicle. Two supports also required for outside corners.
Shovels	Take 2, of the type with pointed blades (entrenching tools).
Spiders	Elastic, for securing everything.
Stove	(See detailed note at end of list).
String	Small ball of strong string.
Tableware	Plates, cups, coffee pot, tea pot etc. China and glass are too fragile, enamel chips, aluminium dents and is difficult to clean, plastic scratches. Chichester stainless steel is my recommendation.
Tape recorder	You may wish to record your expedition on film and sound; but for those who like

music, the desert offers one of the last refuges for musical appreciation, undisturbed by passing aircraft. All such equipment should be most carefully wrapped in polythene bags and carried in a zip-up bag.

Tent pegs	Several spare ones.
Thermometer	The maximum-minimum variety will constantly surprise by the extreme figures registered. The magnet should be attached by string to prevent loss. The shaking it will get may cause the mercury to separate but this can be rectified by means of centrifugal force if the thermometer is swung at arm's length, the mercury end away from you. Start gently and gradually increase speed of swing, watching results repeatedly.
Thermos	You should have 2, size according to number in party. You will want them for hot soup, tea or coffee. Hot drinks are more refreshing than cool ones.
Tin opener	Take 2 because they are easy to lose and there is no substitute.
Toilet	Folding aluminium: can be a great encouragement!
Torch	And spare batteries.
Towels	At least 3 for drying, although paper will do.
Tray	Surprisingly useful, particularly during cooking operations. A big one can be used as toboggan on steep sand dunes.
Umbrella	For use as a parasol, or as a screen in a flat desert in conjunction with a folding toilet! It can even be used as an umbrella—it may rain before you get there.
Washing powder	A litre polythene bottle should suffice for clothes.

Washing-up liquid If used sparingly, as it should be, a small bottle should last.

Water-sterilising tablets (See Chapter 14).

Water heater A 12-volt plug-in immersion heater or kettle, for use while on the move, can save valuable time on arrival. The dangers of boiling water being spilt inside the vehicle should be appreciated.

Wind shield The folding type of aluminium and canvas is useful, particularly for those doing the cooking. Choose bright colours as an aid for signalling.

Stoves

Gas burning unit Most people prefer these; numerous models of single burner, double burner and double with grill units are available. They are trouble-free, clean and quiet. But there is a snag. Refills are not always available and this means taking all you require which represents a lot of extra weight. They are expensive to buy (although they can occasionally be hired) and cannot, therefore, be thrown away when empty, thus providing an additional space problem. It is true that bottled gas of one type or another is widely available throughout Saharan towns of any size, but there are problems with connectors/adaptors and returning the cylinders to the same place. Camping Gaz do provide a list of stockists but appropriate cylinders are not always in stock. Because of these considerations you may like to ponder alternatives, none of them problem-free!

Pressure or Primus Stoves These are fine but most need methylated spirit to preheat them and paraffin to operate them. Both are fuels for which you will have no other requirement and present an additional storage and weight problem, for local supplies of both fuels are uncertain.

Petrol Stoves These have proved my reluctant choice; they can be dangerous and they make a hideous roar which violates the silence of the desert. But since one is already carrying petrol it is the most practical solution in the circumstances, particularly from the point of view of storage and weight. If you do buy a petrol stove, buy a good quality one; an accidental petrol burn in the middle of the desert is a bad thing. Read the instructions very carefully (make sure they are in English before you go) and concentrate on what you are doing whenever you use the stove. Never put your head over it while lighting the stove and be careful not to let anything boil over on it; they can flare up suddenly. If of good quality and sensibly handled, they are safe. For convenience you will need to take a small metal petrol can and a metal filter with fine gauze for refilling.

Camera and films
The following advice has been offered by **Kodak Limited**:

Precautions that the tourist should take during a short stay in a tropical climate.

1. Do not leave the camera in hot sunshine for longer than is necessary and do not leave it in an enclosure which may become very hot, such as the glove compartment or the boot of a car standing in the sun.

2. In a dusty place, keep the camera in its case and the lens capped when not in use. Cap auxiliary lenses at both ends.

3. Some photographers mount a haze filter or a piece of optical glass permanently on the lens as protection against abrasion by dust. A scratched filter can be renewed at moderate cost if necessary. A haze filter has no appreciable effect on exposures.

4. Films are packaged in heat-sealed envelopes for protection against changes in relative humidity. Until you are ready to use them, keep the films in these sealed envelopes.

5. To avoid moisture condensing on film and lens surfaces when you have kept them in an air-conditioned room for some time, allow both film and camera to warm up before using them in a hot and humid atmosphere.

6. When a film has been removed from the moisture-resistant envelope, it is immediately subject to deterioration in a hot or humid climate. Colour films are particularly susceptible in this respect. Consequently, all films should be processed as soon as possible

after exposure. If processing facilities are not available in the vicinity, post the film to the most convenient processing station immediately.

Black-and-white materials withstand moderate heat without serious changes in their characteristics. Colour materials, however, must be kept at temperatures below 55°F (10°C) to retard undesirable changes.

8. An effect of taking photographs when the sun is directly overhead occurs in landscapes without high trees or buildings: the absence of shadow yields a very flat, uninteresting picture. The only way to avoid this result is to photograph the subject either earlier or later in the day when shadows are longer.

This advice is obviously difficult to put into practice in the context of Saharan exploration but it should be followed as far as possible. Remember that for religious or security reasons photographs can arouse sensitivity. It is not unusual for locals to expect a tip if you photograph them.

7

Maps

It is not, I think, until attempting to equip oneself with maps that one is confronted with the uncomfortable realisation that the Sahara has never been really adequately mapped. So used are we to the almost faultless cartography of the travelled world that at first it seems improbable that good Saharan maps do not exist; just that we cannot lay hands on them. Indeed, perhaps they do exist but, if so, they have eluded my grasp, and also that of all Saharan travellers I have so far encountered. So it is as well to reckon without the equivalent of British ordnance survey maps.

In retrospect I sometimes reflect that the imaginative exuberance displayed by the Saharan map makers adds substantially to the individual character of Saharan travel. Journeying all day in expectation of meeting a 'marked earth road', only to find a perfect and absolute blank on the face of the earth, calls for a mental somersault. The immediate reaction of all but the most confident is to conclude that one's navigation is in error and that the elusive road lies just ahead or 'just over there'. But ultimately one is forced to conclude that the spot has indeed been reached and for a while—such is one's faith in the infallibility of modern cartographers—one suspects that the road has become covered in a sand storm or that one was thinking of something else as one drove across it. But no. The road is simply not there and never was.

Many are the traps set for the unwary. A favourite one is to print the symbol for an airport in a rather outlandish place. The greener traveller regards this as such an obvious landmark that, although he may reflect on the curiosity of the location, all worry about overlooking it is swept aside. The cartographer, who has come into possession of some defence map showing possible sites for emergency landings, is laughing quietly for he, unlike you, knows that in reality the surface of the desert is still its pristine self.

It is as well to remember that an empty space on a map is as much of a worry to a map maker as was an empty space on a table in a Victorian house. But having made this unkind observation I will add, paradoxically perhaps, that some maps are a miracle of comparatively accurate information. When one comes to appreciate the difficulties of surveying accurately such a vast and inaccessible landscape, one is full of praise for the relatively small number of errors.

A feature of Saharan maps is that they are essentially idiosyncratic. You need to get the 'feel' of each series. Some insist on showing as main *pistes* camel-caravan tracks scarcely used for fifty years. But the same map may show a concern for the delineation of mountain peaks that another may overlook entirely. Some show the positioning and directional pattern of sand dunes while others just mark the area in yellow, adding a few cross hatchings here and there to give a more authentic effect. A feature common to them all is the marking and naming of oases with an apparent indifference to their nature and size: a prosperous oasis with a thousand or so inhabitants and an oasis deserted years ago are marked similarly.

In a book in which I am largely obliged to confine myself to generalisation or recommendations, it is good to be able to state categorically that, in my view, there is one map which is so much better than all the others that, unless you intend to stray from the marked track, it is the only one worth taking. It is also the cheapest.

Let me introduce the Michelin map, sheet number 153. If

you hear someone say: 'Have you a spare 153?' it is to this that they are referring. It, and its predecessors, have become the classic Saharan maps of recent years. It is also one of the very few which covers the whole Sahara and its approaches. Its scale is 1:4,000,000, which is 63 miles to the inch; sobering to reflect that the map measures about 4ft × 3ft and that in some areas a hard day's driving may take you across little more than an inch of the map. My advice in interpreting this map is not to rely too much on the exact positioning of features; inexactitudes are, in any case, virtually inevitable in a map of this scale. To avoid 'disappointments' it may be as well to downgrade each road classification by one grade. In this way you will be less surprised to find that a 'Trans-Continental Earth Road' is, in fact, a track only possible for four-wheel drive vehicles, or that 'unmarked dirt roads' may not in reality exist at all. Routes marked *'interdite'* are not necessarily forbidden. Water from wells shown as having drinking water should be treated with suspicion. Do not expect features like forts to be anything more than a small pile of stones. And so on. You should be cautious about relying too heavily on a single marked feature, just as you should not be too disconcerted to come to a road or a soaring mountain peak quite unmarked. The conclusion of all this is, nevertheless, that if you are crossing the Sahara take this map if you take nothing else; better still, take two; it is easy to lose one or for it to become torn with use.

For Morocco, there is Michelin number 169. For Northern Algeria and Tunisia, Michelin number 172. Again, these are the best for their respective regions. Adjacent Michelin maps are numbers 154 (North-east Africa) and 155 (Central and South Africa).

A series of maps on twice the scale of Michelin number 153 is the series number 2201, compiled by the Ministry of Defence, London, from US Army maps. The Sahara is covered by nine sheets, numbers 1, 2, 3, 6, 7, 8, 11, 12 and 13, and the majority were brought up to date in 1969. These maps attempt a topographical representation in some detail and are therefore invaluable for non-*piste* exploration but, again, too great a reliance on any feature is an error. I have found them especially good at marking prominent peaks and ridges but they are frankly misleading in their representation of 'roads'.

The best detailed series are those prepared by the Institut Géographique National of Paris. Twice the scale again (1:100,000 or 16 miles to the inch), some 30 maps cover the Sahara, but not all are available and they are not uniform. This is a very good series indeed and my recommendation for off-*piste* travel. An attempt is made to mark almost everything and, due to the number of colours used, the result is quite clear and uncluttered. This series gives by far the best idea of regional topography, but once again you should not treat representation of a road on the map as evidence of its visible existence. The series was last brought up to date in 1961 but this is not a serious drawback.

With this choice of maps it is not worth mentioning any others with the exception, perhaps, of the nearly three-dimensional physical map of the Sahara in the *Reader's Digest World Atlas*. It gives a comprehensive idea of the Saharan land mass. Perhaps also the *Daily Telegraph* map of Africa (1:11,500,000). It is regularly revised and keeps one abreast of changing political situations.

For those who wish to spare no expense, up-to-date aerial photographs taken from satellites are available by negotiation with the Pentagon in Washington. They can cost up to £150 each but can be enlarged to show perfectly clearly an object on the ground the size of a bottle.

The names and addresses of suppliers and approximate costs of the maps mentioned in this Chapter are given in Appendix D.

The following glossary of words (Arab and Tamashek) used on these maps may be of some help. The spelling of these words varies from map to map.

Page 71 TYPES OF SURFACE
13 A party exploring in the Ténéré desert. Smooth hard sand like this gives ideal driving conditions
14 Rock: slow and heavy on tyres but it can be a welcome change from soft sand

15 Digging away sand before inserting sand ladders—note ladder at rear of vehicle

16 The other method!

Maps

Adrar	mountain
Aguelmam	lake
Aguelmane	waterhole
Aguelmanl	small lake
Ain, ayn	spring
Ait	proper name
Ajjer	river
Alama	cairn
Allous	mountain chain
Anou	well
Aqba	slope, col
Atmur	open plain
Auenat	well
Bahár	sea
Bahia	bay
Bahiret	lagoon
Bahr	stream
Baten	slope
Beni	proper name
Bir, Bi'r	well
Bordj	fort
Bou	well
Chebka	hilly area
Chott	playa, lake, salt marsh
Daiet, Daya	wet depression
Darb	road, track
Djamour	island
Djebel	mountain
Dur	plateau, hill
Edehin	sandy plain
Ehi	hill
Embalse	dam
Ensenada	bay
Erg	dunes
'Ezbet	hamlet, settlement
Foumirate	well

Gara, Gára, Gáret, garet	hill
Garaet	depression
Gassi	pass between dunes
Gebel, Gebél	mountain
Ghadir	pool
Ghard	sand dune
Gour(s), Gur	hill(s)
Goz	sand ridge
Guelta	pool, usually permanent
Habit	dry lake
Hamada, Hammadat	stony plain, rocky plateau
Hamadet	rocky barren plateau
Hassi	well, waterhole
'Idd	well
Ilw	rising ground
In, I-n	well
Jabal, Jebel	mountain, hill
Jafjaf, Jef-Jef	cliff
Laguna	lake
Lawdh	hills
Mallahat	salt lake
Mar	sea
Ma'tan	cistern, well
Monti	mountains
Mreyye	mirage area
Nebba	salt well
Oglat	well
Oua-n	well

73

E

Oulad	tribe of (proper name)	Sahra	sand sea
Oum	well	Sarir, Serir	gravel desert
		Serrania	ridge
Penon	rock island	Tarso	plateau, mountain region
		Tassili	stone plateau
Qaltat,	waterhole	Thamad	waterhole, well
Qarar	low area	Tilmas	waterhole
Qàrat,	hill	Tin	summit, éminence
Qarat Qur		Ti-n, Tine	well
Qàryat	village		
Qoz	sand ridge	'Uwaynat	well
Quwayrat	small hill		
		Wadi	water course
		Wilayat	province
Ras	peak, point	Wudayyat	small water course
Reg	rocky ground		
Rhourde	dune	Zahr	escarpment

8

Camping

The Sahara is a camper's paradise. So ideal is it for the purpose that even those who, like myself, do not take to camping in northern latitudes will find themselves adapting to the life with enthusiasm, as though they had done it all their lives.

Because of the difficulty in obtaining them, you will have taken all possible comforts with you. The whole desert is yours from which to choose an ideal and entirely private site; it almost never rains out of season; fires light with the first match; kettles boil almost before you put them down; tent pegs push firmly home. This is my recurrent memory of Saharan camping and it is something of a mental effort to remind myself that there were occasions when not everything in the garden was quite so rosy! It has blown; there have been sand storms, unwelcome visitors, flies, extreme cold and recalcitrant tent pegs. Exceptions, perhaps, but none the less real when they occur.

There is much that can be done to insulate the 'amateur' camper from troubles and I offer the following advice, in so doing claiming for myself a most amateurish status, fairweather camper as I undoubtedly am! Clearly it is important to have the right equipment but, before discussing this in some detail, there are a few general observations to be made.

It is always a good plan to avoid camping in or near an oasis, town or village to escape the attentions of numerous children and not a few adults. They may be curious, mischievous or mendicant. Unless you are infinitely resilient you will not enjoy their attentions, which will include endless staring, touching, pawing, questioning and some demanding. Try to find a place that is hidden from the road, if there is one, and several miles from any human habitation. Otherwise you can be quite certain of a visit. Anywhere inhabited will be infested with flies and other unpleasantnesses. Anywhere with vegetation will have animal life and consequently flies. A general rule is, therefore, that the thicker the vegetation the greater the risk of flies and other creatures whose attentions you may, if you are not studying natural history, wish to avoid in the interest of comfort.

Stop for the night in good time to make sure that your campsite requirements are met. Many a night's rest has been ruined by failure to observe an encampment of nomads a mile or so away and it is a tedious business to repack everything. Another reason for stopping early is to become organised during daylight and to enjoy, in a moment of relaxation, the brief splendours of a desert sunset.

One of the first things to do is forget the artificialities of time. It is a wonderful feeling to rise with the sun, or even half-an-hour earlier while dawn breaks—undeterred that your watch is showing 5.00 am. And you will be refreshed and ready to get up if you went to bed at, say, 9.00 pm.

Your progress depends on how early you manage to break camp. It is all too easy to rise slowly, waiting to be warmed by the sun, and then to become immersed in the routine of washing oneself, one's laundry and the dishes of the previous evening; all this, together with breakfast, a little maintenance and clearing up the campsite, can take three hours. Better far to drive after a prompt breakfast until you halt for the midday meal, by which time you will need a longish break; the heat can, in any event, make driving arduous at this time. But the same heat will by then have warmed the water in the jerrycans enough for washing up or shaving.

It pays great dividends if the interior of the vehicle is kept

tidy and everything put back in its place each morning; few
things are better calculated to irritate than rummaging in the
back of a hot, airless truck.

Campers tend to feel that tasks should be shared and shared
alike, but a good organiser can sometimes manage to get everyone to do the thing at which he is best. For instance, there may
be a born cook or mechanic in the party. By tact, everyone can
be persuaded that the job will benefit greatly from his attention.
But whether you agree with this or not, it unquestionably pays
to arrive at an understanding as to who does what—in default
of this it is surprising how many jobs are overlooked.

When you break camp it is your responsibility to see that the
site is as you found it, with all rubbish properly buried. Remember, though, that things useless to you are sometimes much
appreciated by the natives—an empty gallon plastic oil con-
tainer, for example, makes a good friend of the boy who leads
you to the well in the next oasis.

Although you will certainly need a stove, you will do well to
use an open fire when possible. Contrary to most people's
notion, the Sahara has a great area over which trees grow.
Some of these trees hardly deserve the title since they are only
ten feet or so in height and some areas may support only a few
such trees to a square mile. The fact remains, however, that
beneath Saharan trees you can often very easily collect enough
dead sticks (without removing any branches from the trees
which may have taken years to reach this diminutive size) for
a good fire. You can secure a pile of such sticks on top of the
vehicle with 'spiders' or contained in large baskets.

The snag to the sticks is that most are covered with im-
probably long thorns. But one soon gets used to collecting them
without destroying one's hands, and they produce great heat
quickly, so you do not need a lot. They are normally bone dry
and a single match will ignite quite a large stick. Often such
fires, apart from keeping away flies, provide a wonderful
fragrance, although perhaps the greatest joy is that you are

spared the noise of a pressure stove.

Apart from normal methods of washing up, sand is an excellent cleaner. The greasiest plate will respond to a little water and a handful of sand but this presupposes the use of stainless steel plates.

For washing clothes you can devise a most effective washing machine by suspending a strong fertiliser bag filled with the washing, some water and soap powder, from the roof of the vehicle—or even standing the bag in a bowl on the floor of the vehicle—and just leaving it. Fifty miles of bumping along on the desert *pistes* (or a few hundred yards of 'washboard') will do all that an electric washing machine can do, and at less cost to the clothes.

I have made it a golden rule that after any halt for a meal or for the night, I walk once round the vehicle before climbing aboard. It is amazing how often one sees something left lying on the ground or on the vehicle.

Finally, it should be said that courtesy must be extended towards those you encounter while camping, even if you had hoped to avoid their attentions. Remember that you are an intruder into their country and, however inhospitable the desert may appear to you, the land—or the use of it—may belong to someone.

9

Clothes

The desert can be very cold, as well as very hot, but it is normally dry—although on the way there you may get wet! So in theory you need everything; in practice you will have to simplify your requirements especially if you are travelling by air.

Anything other than casual clothes is normally pointless but, if space permits, you may be glad of a suit or evening dress should you visit one of the better hotels or restaurants in a large town.

Do not try to economise on space or weight by leaving out warm and wind-resistant clothes—though clearly you need less warm clothing in summer than in winter.

Cotton material and loose fitting clothes are much the coolest. Cotton and terylene mixtures are reasonably cool and usually have the great advantage of being drip dry. Nylon should definitely not be worn.

If you are entering mosquito territory you will need long-sleeved shirts and trousers which will tuck into ankle-length boots. Clothes should be packed in polythene bags to protect them from sand, and everything is best packed in holdall-type baggage which is less space-consuming than suitcases.

Suggested clothing list

2 pairs of lightweight trousers (drip dry if possible)	3 shirts (drip dry if possible)
	1 windproof anorak
2 pairs of shorts (or third pair of trousers)	1 thin jersey
	1 thick jersey

2 pairs warm pyjamas/ nightdresses	(suede or leather and comfortable for walking)
3 sets underwear	supply of handkerchiefs or tissues
4 pairs socks/stockings	
1 swimsuit	1 folding plastic raincoat
1 pair sandals or beach shoes	2 towels
1 pair ankle-length desert boots	1 pillow

Some, or all, of the items on the following check-list may be useful:

Airmail paper and envelopes	Moisturising cream
Ballpoint pens and pads	Money belt
Battery shaver/razor and blades	Nail scissors
Books on Sahara	Pastilles (for a dry throat in a hot
Cottonwool/tissues	desert, or boiled sweets though
Hot water bottle—for those who	these can make you thirsty)
rely on them at home and	Personal wash kit, nailbrush
invalids	Soap
'Hussif'	Spare shoelaces
Insect repellent	Suntan lotion
Lip salve (essential)	Talc powder
Moisturised cleansing pads	

The glare from light sand can be at least as strong as the glare from snow so sunglasses may be helpful. If you wear spectacles remember that you can have your prescription made up with tinted lenses. Wearers of contact lenses may find that fine airborne sand is an irritant.

Use vehicle wing mirror for a shaving mirror.

See also Chapters 6, 8 and 14.

10

Provisions and Cooking

Expedition morale largely depends on the success of the meals. Nothing so dampens the spirit as the foreknowledge of unpalatable food. It is extraordinary then to find so little imagination deployed in the field kitchen.

If you are seeing the Sahara with one of the tour companies you will not have to worry about buying or cooking food, though you may have some worries about eating it if the cook is as uninspired as some are. And on occasions you will be eating out—cook's day off—whether you like it or not.

You may be travelling along the tarmac in your own car, perhaps on the northern fringes of the desert, staying at hotels for the night. In this case you are likely to have brought neither extensive provisions nor cooking facilities with you and your main concern will perhaps be providing your own midday meals. Bread, butter, cheese, some tinned food, and fruit are normally found at most larger towns. But if you are moving slowly you may need to take enough food for three or four days. Drinking water need not be a problem in these areas, though it is as well to take plenty in case of breakdown: half a jerrycan a head is not too much.

If you are camping and doing your own catering it is worth organising yourself carefully because a great deal of trouble and discomfort can be saved. However, a lot will depend on the space and weight you can allow for the food and equipment.

For the sake of convenience, health and sometimes cost, you

81

will almost certainly need to equip yourself with a considerable quantity of food. Faced with the prospect of spending a considerable sum, it is very tempting to drive round to a 'cash and carry' or discount shop and make bulk purchases of dozen or two dozen lots, to save money. It is, in my opinion, a cardinal error.

There appears no logical reason why one should become so bored with the same tins in such a very short time. It depends on the tin or the food—I am not sure which—but there are some tinned products which defy one to make a second attempt. Since most people find this to be the case, it results both in hunger and in carting numerous unwanted tins across the desert.

The solution lies either in sampling the products first or in buying small quantities of a greater range of food. Obviously the choice of food rests on the individual tastes of the party and the skills of the cook but it is important to try and achieve a proper nutritional balance. I give below a list of food that was purchased for three people for six weeks. The total weighed 350lb and cost £70. It proved slightly excessive, and several items bought in lots of 6, 9 or 12 would have been better divided into other varieties of similar food:

12	Vichyssoise	3	Steak and Kidney Pie
9	Cream of Scampi	6	Sliced Roast Lamb
2	Cream of Mushroom Soup	6	Sardines
9	Game Soup	3	Canelloni
		4	Minced Beef and Onion
12	Orange Juice	8	Ham Risotto
12	Pineapple	6	Pate de Foie
12	Mandarin Orange	12	Tuna Fish
12	Grapefruit	4	Curried Chicken
12	Pears	8	Sausages
6	Ready cooked Prunes	8	Cods Roes
12	Peeled Tomatoes	2	Anchovies
8	packets Dried Figs	2	Danish Bacon
12	packets Fruit Bars	1	Fish Smokie
4	Hot Dog	6	Tagliatelli

12	Sliced Onions	2lb	Sultanas
9	packets Mashed Potato	1	box Mixed Herbs
4	Sweet Red Peppers	1	Cloves
3	Sauerkraut	4	Bouquet Garni
3	Beansprouts		
7	Potatoes	1	bottle Cooking Oil
6	Beetroot	1	bottle Seasoned Salt
12	Asparagus Spears	1	packet Rock Salt
6	Carrots		Dried Egg
9	Spinach Leaf	1	bottle Lemon Juice
6	Green Beans	1	bottle Vinegar
6	Sweet Corn	1	bottle Olive Oil
1	jar Dried Mixed Peppers		
2	Celery Hearts	2	Danish Camembert
		6	Salted Mixed Nuts
		20	individual Marmalade
100	Tea Bags	1	jar Marmite
4lb	Ground Coffee	1	jar Honey
6	Skimmed Milk	2	jars Parmesan
1	jar Decaffeineated Coffee		
		2	Irish Fruit Cakes
		2	Dundee Cakes
4	packets Long Grain Rice	2	Fruit and Cherry Cakes
2	packets White Sauce	2	Fruit Cakes
8	tubes Tomato Puree	8	packets Crispbread
2lb	Self-raising Flour	10	packets Biscuits

Quantities given in tins unless otherwise stated

This list made an allowance for a small quantity of food to be bought locally. In fact, I recommend travellers to leave at least thirty per cent of their requirements for local purchase. Not only does this make for a welcome variation from packet food but gives a better diet. Fresh vegetables and fruit are, and taste, far better than tinned. Prices too are often less than the preserved equivalent, and it makes a considerable saving on weight. Making local purchases can be great fun and provides an opportunity to use the market places of the Sahara—sources of the greatest fascination and colour.

Local shopping does, of course, leave something to chance. The uncertainties of distribution are great and much depends on luck. The quantities of vegetables available for sale in an oasis are very small—just enough for the few people able to afford them. In great heat vegetables do not last long and only small quantities are taken to market. So, by the time you arrive, they may all have gone. However, because of the scarcity and cost of transport, locally grown produce often appears as a glut. Sound advice is to buy what you see while it is there—you may never see it again.

It is difficult to give a guide to Saharan markets, but it is safe to assume that during the long growing season you will find vegetable produce: potatoes, tomatoes, turnips, radishes, lettuces, cornsalad, spinach, *côte-de-bête*, beetroot, artichokes, onions, beans, lentils, cabbage, marrows, carrots, celery and aubergines, to name some. Again, according to season: apples, pears, figs, pomegranates, apricots, olives, oranges, limes, lemons, mangoes, melons, strawberries, pineapples, coconuts, dates and always a selection of nuts, herbs and spices, many of them exciting new finds for most Europeans. Meat exists but, except in the largest towns, is of doubtful quality. Camel is eaten widely and is quite tender. Flour is also plentiful.

Dairy produce is very scarce (excepting tins of condensed milk)—cow's milk is a rarity and in spite of the incredible number of Saharan goats and camels, their milk is not plentiful, nor is goat's cheese. But yoghurt is common and is almost always good. Butter is found only in large towns and tinned butter will turn liquid as soon as you arrive in the hot desert. Jam and honey are scarce and expensive. Wine—which demonstrates a surprising ability to withstand a severe shaking —can be purchased in north Africa very cheaply. Beer is available almost everywhere in the main centres.

It may well be that only two or three items are available together in one place, so you cannot count on topping up the larder in an orderly fashion. Even so, for the reason given, I think it is far preferable to rely on a reasonable supply of such foods.

It is worth giving some attention to easily produced cold meals at midday as you are unlikely to feel like hot food. Such things as sardines or tunny fish are excellent but thought needs to be given to providing adequate alternative menus. It is no bad idea for the expedition's cook to prepare menus for at least a two-week period; without careful planning, repetitions are surprisingly difficult to avoid.

Another thought, even if a gloomy one, is to foresee the possibility of upset stomachs and to include something suitable for the invalid of the moment—hot Marmite, for instance. Do not forget that nights can be very cold, and nothing is more warming than hot soup.

Finally, bread. Some people take huge supplies of biscuits and varieties of crispbread to make up for a supposed dearth of fresh bread. In fact, it is widely available (mainly resembling French bread), the quality is usually good and sometimes excellent. Towns and oases of any size are sure to have fresh supplies daily. If it is wrapped in a polythene bag immediately after purchase and kept out of the sun it will easily keep for twenty-four hours. Thereafter you will have to produce your own—it is not the problem it sounds! And even if it is not quite the bread you are used to, it will shortly seem an improvement on crispbread.

This is how to make bread in the manner of the desert Arab. Light a small fire (see note on fires in Chapter 8), having dug a shallow depression for the purpose. Mix plain flour, water and a little salt together to form a pliable dough. This should be thoroughly kneaded to drive out all the air and the resultant lump should form a kind of squashed ball about six or seven inches wide and about three thick. Great care should be taken to see that the outside is perfectly smooth as sand will penetrate all cracks and crevices.

With the aid of your shovel, lift off what by now should be mainly glowing ashes and scoop away the sand immediately below the fire. Place the dough in position (see diagram) and cover with a little hot sand and ashes. Replace the ashes and leave for about ten minutes. Remove the ashes again, turn the dough over and once again replace the ashes, adding some extra sticks to maintain a good temperature. Leave for about twenty-five minutes and the desert-Arab loaf is cooked. A little heavy and the odd grain of sand stuck to the outside, perhaps, but very acceptable for all that.

Eating out

It would be a great pity, to my mind, to make an expedition to the Sahara without sampling the local fare. Nonetheless, it has to be admitted that my reasons for so doing are scarcely gastronomic. The restaurants of the Sahara, generally speaking, are extremely simple both in comfort and choice of food. It must also be faced that to eat at them entails some risk of subsequent stomach upset and this can range from nothing more serious than 'travellers' stomach' to something much worse. Even so, my advice is to take the risk here and there— your chances of being seriously upset are not all that great provided you avoid dangerous foods. These are unbottled water (and ice-cubes), milk, ice-cream, watercress and green salad. All food should be well and recently cooked. All fruit and tomatoes should be peeled. Do not eat under-done meat or fish. These comments apply, of course, equally to locally purchased produce intended for your own camp kitchen. Unpeeled fruit and vegetables, such as lettuce, intended to be eaten raw should be sterilised by chlorination.

Eating out is another opportunity to see how people live—not that any restaurant will be patronised by the poor and the poor constitute the vast majority of the Saharan population. You may rub shoulders with a *pétrolier* (a long-distance petrol tanker driver), a soldier, or an itinerant vendor of hair pomade, and through the medium of the French language discover something of their life and habits. It is sobering to reflect that the food you will be offered will represent luxury to the locals and, however simple it appears to you, you can surmise that the man in the street outside has just had a little millet, some compressed dates cut from a block, and a little sweet tea. You should therefore refrain from criticising what is offered to you—the probability is that because of the colour of your skin you will have been offered the very best in the house; politely decline the foods it is wiser to avoid.

If eating out does not sound wildly exciting you can be fairly sure that it will have a greatly enhanced allure after a week or two of eating from tins. Places you would not think of entering during your first days become objects of gastronomic pilgrimage in due course.

I have not mentioned the Europeanised hotels of luxury or semi-luxury standards, such as those of Morocco or Tunisia. In the best of these it is possible to eat very well and in Morocco especially the national cuisine contains some delectable specialities which, at their best, would rank favourably on the highest tables of Europe.

What to eat

In the poorer parts of the Sahara which, geographically speaking, is most of it, you will only exceptionally be offered a choice of food. But around the fringes the food is influenced by that of adjacent countries.

It is on account of the dishes available along the northern fringe of the desert that one can justify space devoted to regional disher.

The best known dish is *cous-cous*. This is a form of semolina mixed with water and a little oil. It is cooked in steam in a *cous-cousier* (objects seen in every market). Also cooked concurrently in the *cous-cousier* are a variety of diced vegetables, principally turnips, carrots, baby marrows, aubergines, tomatoes, onions and chick-peas. To this mixture is added some meat—beef, mutton or chicken. It is served hot, together with the liquid from the vegetables and, sometimes, a hot chilli sauce. At its best it is delicious.

Méchoui is almost as famous as *cous-cous* and its preparation is something of a rite. A barbecued sheep is cooked slowly over hot embers, basted with butter. It is served on a copper dish, and the participants take the meat with their fingers.

Chakchouka is a dish of peppers and tomatoes in a sauce made of garlic, onions, red peppers and olive oil. It is sometimes served with an egg. *Kebab* is often served with potatoes instead of rice; *dolma* with more spices and herbs than its Greek counterpart and not always wrapped in a vine leaf. A very good dish is *lham lahlou* consisting of mutton and prunes, flavoured with cinnamon and orange flowers. *Bourek* looks like a cigar. It consists of flaky pastry which contains a meat stuffing mixed with onion and fried eggs. *Chorba* is an excellent soup—a meat and vegetable bouillon into which vermicelli, or crushed wheat, is put at the last moment. All over North Africa are excellent *patisseries* often incorporating ingeniously devised combinations of almonds, dates and honey; choose those which appear inaccessible to flies.

Mint tea deserves a reference on its own. It is not only extremely good but the occasion for a ceremony. A great deal of unnecessary rudeness is perpetuated by European visitors who do not appreciate that the offering of tea—however casual —is fundamental to Arab hospitality. The time it takes to

SAHARAN
FEATURES

17 A camel cara-
van assembling
at Bilma to
carry locally
produced blocks
of salt

18 One of Berliet
balises or desert
route-markers
—note the total
absence of
horizon

19 A rock pool or
guelta in the
Tassili moun-
tains; such pools
are seldom dry

20 Low sand
dunes; their
virgin surface
exerts a strong
pull towards
their exploration

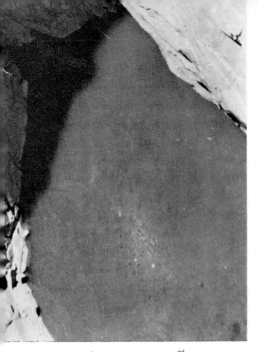

SAHARAN
FEATURES

21 Djado, a
deserted
Saharan oasis

22 A desert loaf
—baking bread
in the sand

23 An orange
glut in a
northern oasis

24 Queueing for
petrol in Djanet;
note the
predominance
of Land-Rovers

produce the tea and the very small glasses into which it is poured often encourage visitors to leave as soon as possible after the first tiny glass has been offered and drunk. It is important to realise that the ceremony consists of drinking *three* glasses and that the intervals between the glasses are intended for conversation. Even if you are offered tea by a desert Arab it will be in the name of ordinary hospitality. At the end of the ceremony and before taking your leave you may like to return the hospitality by presenting a small gift brought for the purpose. But beware of being caught for a tea-drinking ceremony by a Souk stall-holder who will simply be competing for your custom.

F

11

Desert Driving

Tarmac roads

Most tarmac roads are of recent construction and the surfaces correspondingly good. They present few hazards other than those associated with maintaining high speeds over roads which can be extremely hot. Tyre pressures may rise alarmingly and tyres which are not in good condition may cease to conceal the fact. Because many of these new tarmac roads are straight and level there is a temptation to drive too fast.

There are a few points to bear in mind on such roads. Sudden, quite inexplicable, deep potholes occasionally interrupt one's progress with sufficient violence to ensure that a steady lookout is maintained for the next one. Similarly, there are areas where sand drifts across the road in bars. Some of these bars are soft, but others are as hard as iron and it is wise to assume that they will be hard until they have proved soft. Surface widths are variable and on the narrower, single file, roads it is obviously necessary to be ready for traffic coming the other way. Occasionally such traffic consists of heavy lorries which assume some kind of priority and remain firmly in the centre of the single width. Usually these roads are provided with hard shoulders, but sometimes these are not so hard and your speed on approaching an oncoming vehicle should allow for this.

Piste

A road which does not have a tarmac surface is usually referred to as a *piste*, the French for track. *Pistes* can be of two categories: 'improved' and 'unimproved'. The former is usually graded, sometimes provided with markers and, on occasion, such 'works' as bridges and culverts. 'Unimproved' *pistes* tend to be recognisable mainly by virtue of the tracks left by previous users though many are marked with *balises*—the French for markers or cairns.

Mapmakers go to great trouble to differentiate between improved and unimproved tracks but, in practice, the distinction may be meaningless. The actual surface may be far better on an unimproved track because although it may have been graded, an improved track may not be adequately maintained. Tracks which suffer damage from heavy rain and heavy traffic may be almost unusable.

The maintenance of these *pistes* is irregular. Some countries may maintain them in principle, but a national setback such as a drought may cause a total cessation of such work. Political factors are often involved. The indecent haste with which Algeria is applying tarmac to the trans-Saharan *piste* is sometimes ascribed to military considerations. Many of the interior *pistes* owe their existence to the *petroliers*, the great tankers which transport fuel across the Sahara. But a change in policy may mean that Niger, for example, ceases to buy petrol from Libya. Overnight a relatively frequented route may be virtually abandoned. Such *pistes*, if unmarked, can easily disappear after a few sand storms.

For these reasons it is better to ask, where possible, the advice of local police or returning travellers rather than place blind faith in a map.

Corrugated surfaces (washboard)

No amount of maintenance, it seems, eliminates the condition known as 'washboard'—a succession of small undulations or corrugations. These exist throughout the Sahara and come in all sizes. The smallest are scarcely noticeable and merely produce a vibration; the biggest can spell death to saloon cars and are a major hazard even to the largest lorries. An 'average' corrugation might be about three or four feet long and three to six inches deep. The illustration on page 54 shows a lightly corrugated surface. The secret of driving over such surfaces is to go as fast as possible. At about 45 or 50mph the vehicle skims across the tops and gives a comparatively smooth ride, though reaching this speed can be somewhat agonising. But many vehicles cannot achieve this speed, or the nature of the road does not permit it. In this case there is really no option but to go very slowly, although this is fatiguing and most uneconomical with fuel.

Such washboard tracks sometimes continue for only a matter of yards, but they may go on for a great many miles. When travelling over them at speed the greatest care needs to be taken, since there is little contact between the wheels and the surface. The braking efficiency will be much reduced and if the brakes are applied suddenly there is a tendency to skid. The steering wheel needs to be held firmly and a keen lookout is vital. It is often due to the need to drive at speeds over washboard that springs and axles are broken—a dry gully crossing the *piste* may be invisible until too late.

If you encounter such surfaces you will frequently see that alternative tracks exist parallel to the main *piste* and these, being newer, may be less corrugated.

Divergent tracks

A situation much exploited by the cartoonist is that of the desert traveller racked with indecision on encountering a fork with no sign and with both arms of the fork appearing to enjoy equal use.

Such situations do in fact occur rather often. Frequently one track is simply a newer route avoiding washboard, perhaps, and you may very well find that after a period the two tracks join up again. Sometimes, however, it is because of the existence of some habitation unmarked on the map. It often pays to travel a short way down each arm. Usually it becomes clear which is the main track. If it does not, and you are unable to derive help from the compass, all you can do—other than wait for another traveller—is to make a note of the mileage and take your choice. Occasionally you can gain a clue from the width and type of tyre tracks. You may see that heavy lorries go one way and lighter vehicles the other, suggesting perhaps that the track used by lorries may not be the one for you.

The open desert

One of the amazing things about the Sahara is the diversity of surface. You can drive over sand and gravel all day and scarcely encounter two identical stretches. Each surface has its peculiarities and although much is learned from experience, it is seldom safe to assume too much.

So, what rules are there? Very few, in my opinion. When the exceptions become too numerous, the rule may cease to be a rule; thus it is with surfaces of sand and gravel, particularly sand. No two people will agree in their 'reading' of surface characteristics any more than they will agree in their recommendations on how to tackle them. So, no rules but a few generalisations.

Gravel

I start with gravel because it is usually more predictable than sand. It comes in all sizes—so small that it is almost sand and so big that it is almost boulders. But the classic pebble desert, of which there is a great deal, is a generally even surface of small flattish pebbles and is an ideal driving surface. Normally it is consistently firm and safe. Sometimes, though, what appears to be pebble-strewn desert may, in reality, be but a scattering of pebbles over soft sand with the characteristics of soft sand. Pebble surfaces sometimes give way to rocky surfaces which can be very tough on tyres, having sharp angular corners which dig into rubber and are the special enemy of the floatation tyres like Michelin XS.

Sand

The permutations in the size, colour, surface and density of sand are quite astonishing. At its safest it is as fine as baby powder. Running through a bar of such sand across a metalled road can be noticeable only by the variation in sound. But the bar can just as easily be as unyielding as rock and, as mentioned, the general recommendation is to treat sand as being hard if you are expecting it to be soft, and *vice versa*.

The most magnificent driving conditions can be provided by the smooth and firm areas where you can hear the tyres singing on the sand, where you can aim in any direction and drive for miles without hint of vibration. Then, suddenly, you are betrayed. Your mounting confidence is shattered when, apparently without warning, you find your car rapidly slowing and before you have had time to turn you have ploughed to a halt, the tyres sunk deep. You saw absolutely nothing to indicate the change from hard to soft sand. A vehicle perhaps twenty yards to your side remained on hard standing. Such treachery is not unusual but there are some indications which may help you avoid the experience.

In the first place, if you are driving on sand bearing the tracks of other vehicles, you will probably see deeper ruts indicating a patch of soft sand. It is then just a matter of observation to see where the tracks have remained constant. Or you may be changing from the windward to the leeward side of a slope. In principle, most dunes have a hard packed side and a soft reverse side; to some extent this is true for even comparatively slight undulations. So when changing slopes be on the lookout for trouble. Sometimes there is a very slight, almost imperceptible, variation in the colour; do not worry whether it is light on dark, or dark on light—variations are an indication of change. It may just be an alteration of angle toward the sun but it could be a differing texture showing itself.

Sand often forms a crust and, as with skating on thin ice or water skiing, if you go fast enough you remain on the surface; it is only when you slow up or stop that you fall. You can drive happily for miles on such crusts and it is not until you stop and get out that you notice the wheels have become embedded in the last few yards. This is why the desert rats have become accustomed to the sight of an assortment of vehicles racing round and round one stationary one, waiting for it to be dug out. It is a good idea to open the door as you slow down and lean out to watch for the least sign of a failing crust. If you start to sink you should accelerate and try again a few hundred yards away. Try to roll to a halt rather than braking.

On open desert it is usually wise to avoid driving in the tracks of another vehicle because it may well have weakened or broken the crust. If you want to cross existing tracks, take them at a sharp angle—it only requires a few feet of soft sand to halve your speed. Some of the 'mysterious' patches of soft sand are really the former tracks of vehicles which have been levelled up by windborne sand. One often hears of people reducing the tyre pressures in a belief that the flattened tyre gives better traction. The beneficial effect is minimal and to reduce the pressure below 15psi is to risk having the hub rotate without the tyre.

However, many much-used tracks consist of soft sand that is being constantly churned up by traffic. Under such conditions it may be wiser to travel on the most packed sand, such as the tracks of a heavy lorry. But only trial and error can confirm this.

One of the main hazards of driving in the desert is the disappearance of shadows when the sun climbs to its zenith around the middle of the day—I say *around* the middle of the day since it seems to spend as disproportionate an amount of time overhead as it does in rising and setting. Substantial undulations then seem quite without form and I have even known someone fail to see, and drive straight into, the side of a large

sand dune. It is necessary to drive cautiously under these conditions; travel fast enough to stay on the surface but not so fast
that serious damage will result from taking small obstacles too
fast. Speeds will depend on the conditions, but this could mean
35mph instead of 55mph.

As mentioned earlier, crossing washboard can be a gruelling
experience. However, it will be seen that usually these ripples
have a directional uniformity and the jarring effect is sometimes
reduced if one takes them as indicated in the diagram below,
although this obviously reduces progress.

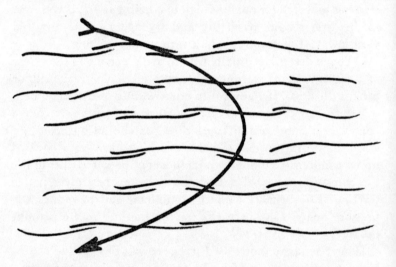

The ultimate promotion for a sand ripple is to become a sand
dune. Dunes have an endless and unique fascination, but for
the driver all but the most junior dunes are to be avoided,
except by experts. Most dunes have a sharp ridge along their
crests and often one side is steeper than the other. To drive up
the less sloping, hard-packed side and tumble over the top on
to a steep fall of soft sand can very easily end in a disastrous roll
to the bottom. A driver stupid enough to do this without first
prospecting on foot deserves the odd roll but, just occasionally,

a longish slope of sand can turn out to be a dune. Suddenly there is a crest, a jolt, and a sheer drop. Should you inadvertently become aware of this too late, all you can do is steer straight down the steepest slope and avoid braking at all costs. In this way, you reduce the chances of the whole vehicle rolling sideways or end-over-end. Dune hopping for the expert can be exhilarating, but it can hardly be called cruising.

Wet sand is another matter. Although some remains firm like beach sand, the general rule is to avoid obviously wet patches, such as one often sees near oases. Avoid, too, the dry areas next to them; the sand just under the surface may be damp and should be given a wide berth. The exception is if you are on a *piste*, in which case stick to it. There are areas of soft sand which may become firm after rain. However, it is unlikely to have just rained and, to give a tip, the going will be firmer early in the morning after the dew has fallen.

Wadis and salt deserts

However strong the wind or the desirability of concealment you should never park or camp in a wadi, irrespective of how dry they may appear or how fine the weather. A storm out of your sight and earshot can cause floods of a sensational character. Wadis can suddenly be the beds of swirling torrents which carry all before them. In a matter of minutes the rushing water can become an impassable obstacle, so it is usually wise to make camp on the far side of the wadi, just in case.

Finally, there are salt deserts. These often announce themselves by the glint of salt crystals in the sun or a streak of water in an otherwise empty stretch of sand. Some of these areas are very treacherous and your vehicle could sink deeply into them. If in doubt avoid them or, at least, prospect on foot.

Navigation

The problem of driving in a wide expanse of desert is largely a navigational one, provided you already know that the surfaces are suitable for your transport. A local guide will usually navigate by memory or instinct. But however good you may think your sense of direction, you will probably be totally lost in quite a short time if you are unable to navigate.

Nor is it safe to assume that, if lost, it is necessary only to retrace your tracks. A sand storm can extinguish them or they may become confused with others. Leaving pieces of paper held by stones may be better than nothing, but if a few consecutive pieces are missing you may easily lose your way.

There is really no alternative to the established methods of navigation. These are not entirely simple and those planning to cruise the open desert should learn thoroughly how to use the equipment before setting out. A good piece of navigational equipment in the desert is the sun compass which can be mounted on the offside wing. The principle is for the driver to maintain the shadow cast by a central spike always in the same place. The compass rose needs to be reset every ten or fifteen minutes to allow for the sun's movement. Although for accurate navigation there is no substitute for the sextant, a good car compass correctly compensated before departure can be a simple or practical aid. Astral navigation is not of great help (unless travelling by camel) since it is generally considered unsafe to drive after dark.

Convoy travelling

When several vehicles are travelling together, the speed of the convoy must be dictated by the speed of the slowest vehicle or driver. It is most unwise to allow faster vehicles to go ahead, even when travelling in groups. If this practice is allowed it is only a matter of time before you find, on reaching your destination, that the others are not there. Neither party will have any idea as to the other's whereabouts. Also, in the event of breakdown, you may need to transfer the passengers and even the load into all available vehicles.

In the event of breakdown, you should switch on the headlights and leave them on. Even in the brilliant desert light this signal can be seen from a great distance.

You may wish to travel well spread out because of the dust raised. To guard against losing a member of the convoy and to ensure that breakdown signals are observed, it is best to establish an order of travel and for each driver to know which vehicle he should keep an eye on.

Mileages

It is always a good practice to note mileages at the start of the day or when passing a landmark. In the event of a forced return, the relevant calculations on fuel and time can then be made.

Solo or in convoy?

This is largely a matter of commonsense—a question of weighing up the consequences of a breakdown. If you are using a well-frequented *piste* you are unlikely to suffer more than inconvenience. But some tracks may only have a few, if any, vehicles in a year and to travel solo under such conditions is clearly extremely foolhardy. You risk losing your own and your passengers' lives and causing major inconvenience and expense in the event of a search party. The same comment must apply to those who travel a 'short way off' the *piste* and then get lost. Certain countries—Algeria for instance—actually categorise the roads according to whether they can be travelled solo or not. You may also be required to obtain permission to use desert tracks. Permission normally means applying to the *mairie* or *daira*, but police permission may be required too. If you do not reach the destination within a reasonable period of your forecast or if you fail to check in, a search may be organised, the costs of which will be your liability.

If this question is being considered at the planning stage a point that is discussed in the section on spares in Chapter 3 should be borne in mind. If several vehicles of the same kind are travelling in convoy there is obviously a greatly reduced need to carry a wide selection of spare parts.

Digging out

When driving over open desert as well as on sandy *pistes*, you are almost certain to find yourself stuck sooner or later. The normal sequence of events that overtakes a novice is a swift loss in forward speed, caused by the soft sand, and a change into a lower gear just before forward speed is lost, causing traction to be sacrificed at the most crucial moment. The vehicle settles, and in a desperate effort to get unstuck the driver accelerates hard. The wheels spin and the vehicle sinks to the axles. A good half-hour's digging is then required before freedom—usually brief—is regained. This situation is not infrequently caused by 'helpfully' driving alongside a vehicle which is already bogged.

It may sound obvious but the best thing is to avoid becoming *really* stuck. There is a moment, a very precise one, when it is necessary to decide whether to abandon the attempt at forward movement. If you realise that you are swiftly sinking, it will pay to stop dead. You may then be able to step out, place the sand ladders (see below) in front of the wheels and drive gaily out to *terra firma* without any digging at all. But some acquaintance with various types of sand, the vehicle concerned and the degree of 'stick' will be necessary before an appropriate judgement can be made.

However, let us assume that you are stuck to the point where digging is necessary. The first thing is to decide whether to come out forwards or backwards. If you are on a narrow track it may be absolutely necessary to go forwards if you cannot afterwards go round the obstacle. But if on open ground you should see, by walking around, which offers the best hope. If on a slope it will probably be easiest to go down it—even a slight slope makes a surprising difference.

Assuming you are going out forwards, whether in a two or four-wheel drive vehicle, it is necessary to remove sand from in front of all four wheels. Again, knowing the amount to remove will depend on your experience. In more severe cases sand should be removed from the sides of the wheels as well, since the frictional hold which such sand exerts can deprive you of the power you need to extricate yourself.

In the most severe cases, where the chassis touches the sand, you must either dig away underneath, which is an unspeakable exertion, or clear just enough to enable you to place the jack beneath the front (or rear) axle. Of course the jack must be placed firmly on a suitable base, say two lengths of 4in × 4in timber, 2ft long. Then, with a few strokes of the handle the front (or rear) is well up and ladders can be placed beneath the wheels. It will probably be unnecessary to repeat the performance with the other end. (Do not forget to remove the jack!)

Digging in the heat is to be avoided where possible; it is extremely exhausting and should never be tackled savagely. With a temperature of 110°F or so a frenzied series of digs can end in serious exhaustion. Read in the cool temperatures of our island it sounds ludicrous to suggest that every superfluous movement should be avoided but you will be surprised, however fit you are, by the speed at which you become exhausted in such conditions.

Sand ladders

Two sand ladders are absolutely necessary in one form or another. Lorries usually carry long sections of steel channel or some kind of mesh. Some people arrive with sacks or pieces of carpet but these are quite useless. The principle of the ladder is to get you up on the crust again and since obviously anything flexible cannot achieve this, supports must be strong enough to remain rigid under the weight of the vehicle. The ladders should be a minimum of 4ft long, preferably 5ft, and be stowed so that they can be removed rapidly and easily.

To emerge forwards in a four-wheel drive vehicle, it is best to place the ladders before the front wheels. If deeply embedded, you will need to dig away sufficiently to be able to place the ladders so that the wheels will climb on to them. The point about putting them at the front end is that they will then serve for the rear wheels as soon as they have passed under the front ones. Similarly, if you are attempting to come out backwards, they should be placed behind the rear wheels. In a two-wheel drive vehicle they should, of course, be placed in front of the driving wheels.

It is a good idea to attach a few feet of strong cord to the ladder ends (leaving the cords lying at right angles to the ladders) for, after they have been driven over, the ladders may be six inches or so under the sand. To retrieve them you can then pull the cord which saves some prodding with a spade. Some people suggest tying long lengths of cord to the ladders with the other ends attached to the vehicle. However, I do not recommend this as, if the ladders are deeply buried, the cord will break unless it is extremely strong. Alternatively, if the cord is strong enough, the sudden extra drag caused by the buried ladders may be enough to bring the emergent and still struggling vehicle to a premature halt. Nevertheless, in default of such an arrangement, it means that a passenger has to be left to extract the ladders and walk forward with them.

Once the digging has been completed and the ladders aligned with the vehicle, you are ready to come out. You will probably need the lowest gear and all the power you have. In a Land-Rover this means first gear, low ratio and plenty of engine revolutions when you let in the clutch; it is hard on the clutch and this is why a good one is necessary. Accelerate as hard as you can whilst still on the ladders and, if possible, change into second to regain as much speed as quickly as possible.

Needles to say, once on the move, you will not stop until you are certain of being on firm ground, despite the wails of the passenger reclaiming the sand ladders! Some travellers recommend unrolling wire netting, 18 inches wide by 20 feet long in front of the sand ladders. However, I do not consider this very practical, especially with a heavy vehicle, as the wire netting tends to get into a terrible mess very quickly!

Towing out

If another vehicle is nearby on firm ground it may be simple to get yourself towed out, though often this results in both vehicles becoming stuck. It is perhaps better to remain independent as long as possible.

Winching out

The merits of winches in general are discussed in Chapter 3 in the section on choosing a Land-Rover. If you or another accompanying vehicle have a winch, extraction is again a simple matter, provided there is firm standing for the second vehicle within the length of the winch cable and in the appropriate direction. A very strong shackle should be used as the link between the towing eye and the winch cable hook; if the shackle is weak it will bend and the pin become jammed. Remember to keep bystanders away from an area equivalent to the length of the cable in every direction in case the cable fractures. Very serious injury can result from the whiplash of a broken cable.

If you have a winch but are unaccompanied, you need to provide yourself with an anchor for the other end of the cable. Rocks and trees are seldom available within a suitable distance of patches of soft sand, and the most convenient object is likely to be your spare wheel. Roll this forward to a point just short of the unwound cable end. Dig a hole for the wheel, leaving a longish channel for the cable so that its angle is as low as possible, as in the diagram overleaf. Replace the sand and operate the winch gently. If you are in luck the vehicle will emerge from its hole toward the spare wheel; if you are not the reverse will occur—and a very depressing sight it presents. This operation looks easier than it is; digging an adequate hole in soft sand and in great heat is not really practical. The surrounding sand keeps filling the hole, especially from the place where you are standing. It should be regarded as a last resort apart from pushing which, though exhausting, is the most effective way of getting out of soft sand; indeed, if there are half a dozen pairs of strong hands available this is often the quickest way out of trouble.

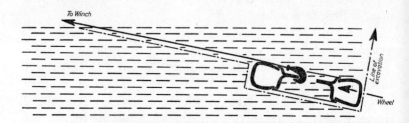

If your vehicle is not fitted with a winch, a practical alternative is a self-hauling device. This can be easily manufactured locally; it consists of drums mounted on the rims of both rear wheels and secured with a few wheel bolts. Both ends of a strong tow rope are attached to the drums. A pulley or, better still, two pulleys are secured to a tree or to a ground anchor driven into the sand some distance from the vehicle and the vehicle can then pull itself out of the sand when the rope winds itself round the drums.

General

Select the gear appropriate to the terrain. You will not save petrol by straining the engine in too high a gear.

Avoid overheating by avoiding engine strain. Keep engine revolutions up. In an emergency you can improve matters by turning on the heater (you will hardly notice the extra heat!) removing the thermostat and putting a rag round the fuel pump/filter/carburettor which should be 'connected' to the windscreen washer so that it can be kept wet.

Drive through the oases with exaggerated care; do not expect people or animals to make a path for you and do not rely on the horn—its use may be resented.

Page 107
SAHARAN
FEATURES
25 Wind-sculp-
tured rocks
such as this
are to be
found in
numerous
parts of the
desert
26 Rossi, a
Tuareg guide,
leans against
the Tree of
Ténéré, per-
haps the most
famous tree in
the world. It
stands alone in
the scorching
Ténéré desert
beside two
deep wells and
is the subject
of many myths

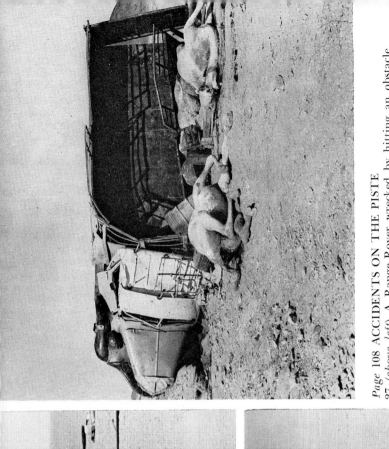

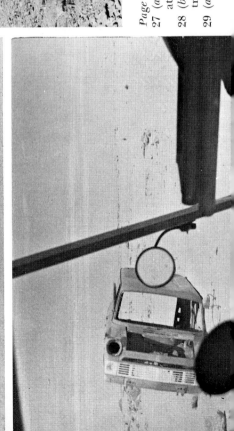

Page 108 ACCIDENTS ON THE PISTE

27 (*above left*) A Range-Rover wrecked by hitting an obstacle at high speed

28 (*below left*) One of the numerous burnt-out wrecks by the trans-Saharan *piste*—each one the end of an expedition

29 (*above*) The end of a trans-Saharan lorry—and its load

12

Fauna and Flora

Fauna

The mythology of the Sahara is incomplete without enormous hairy monsters and fiery snakes. Alas, I have to say that, even if once prevalent, such creatures are now extinct.

The existence of much animal life in the desert seems somehow unlikely. How, one asks, could anything survive the merciless conditions? However, relatively little of the desert is completely devoid of plant life and wherever there is vegetation there is bound to be animal life. The richer the vegetation the more life it will harbour and the oases are not only islands of plant life but the habitat of many animal species.

The manner in which desert animals have adapted themselves to their environment is fascinating. The main factors influencing the type of species found are the vegetation, temperature extremes, dryness, hours of sunshine and so on. Complicated systems have been evolved for conserving body moisture yet at the same time regulating temperature. Many animals have adopted a nocturnal activity to spare them the need to withstand the killing temperatures of midday. Any animal smaller than a hare has to burrow into cool sand during the hottest hours, while birds and reptiles remain motionless in a shady spot. Throughout the hottest months of June to September, reptiles aestivate just as in Britain they hibernate during the coldest months.

Many insects behave in the same way, scurrying about their business during the dark hours.

Much of the desert fauna has camouflage colouring; mammals have developed particularly large eyes and ears. Many birds walk more than they fly. All the true desert fauna can survive long periods without water; in fact, some thirty species of reptiles, birds and mammals are known to be more or less independent of water for their entire lives.

Creatures now associated with Central Africa including many of those depicted in the rock paintings such as the elephant, the hippopotamus, the giraffe and the white rhinoceros have disappeared, albeit comparatively recently. It is true, though, that some species can still be found in remote areas where vegetation is relatively plentiful, like the Aïr and Tibesti Mountains. Of the tropical species, one still finds honey badgers, striped weasels, ratels, caracals, servals, panthers and leopards along the northern fringe of the desert; various species of fish, mostly perch, are found in the oases. Equally, there are still some descendents of Ice Age refugees from Europe. They include house mice, rats, red foxes, some species of bat, whitethroats, great tits, turtle doves, barn owls, the common and horned viper and some frogs and toads.

Among the true desert animals are three types of antelope, the addax and the oryx (both very rare), Barbary sheep or moufflon, the fennec—a small sand-coloured fox often to be found tamed and a major carrier of rabies—the larger and rarer sand fox, jackals, striped hyenas, the desert jerboa which resembles the kangaroo rat, and the desert gerbil which is sold in pet shops in Britain. Among the birds are many species of lark, desert bullfinch, bustard, grouse, wheatear and bee-eater. Of the reptiles we find mastigures, chameleons, varans, agamis, skinks, geckos, lizards, horned vipers, sand vipers and sand boas. I will conclude this list by mentioning the existence of forty species of praying mantis, sixty species of scorpion, and several thousand species of desert beetle; it will give some idea of the diversity of the Saharan fauna.

There are people who, on spying some gazelle, consider it

'sporting' to chase them from their vehicle until the gazelle drop exhausted, and then to butcher them. In terms of the conservation of a declining species it represents the most serious threat—stocks have been repeatedly decimated. In terms of 'sportsmanship' such action is cowardly, cruel and totally contemptible.

Flora

To those who expect to find an endless sea of sand, one of the most intense pleasures of the desert is the sudden encounter in an arid and desolate area of a beautiful plant in full flower. Except for the sand seas there is comparatively little desert which does not contain some plant life.

The number of flowers you see will depend not only on where you are but when you are there. After a period of rain the desert can burst into bloom and some of these flowers are glorious. It is a wonderful place for observing the adaptive habits of plants. Under the most inhospitable conditions they have evolved survival and defensive systems of a spectacular kind.

You will observe the most extensive root structures which not only provide the means for water forage but anchor the plant in soft sand and prevent it being blown away in the shelterless desert. Much of the land surface has a high salt content which would kill ordinary plants, so species have adapted themselves to cope with this. The succulents, plants with small leaves or spikes, have evolved these devices to avoid losing moisture or to withstand attack from hungry animals, or both.

Trees of the type seen in an English park do not exist outside the oases. Nonetheless, there are numerous areas where a sprinkling of stunted or dwarfed trees grow. Tamarisks with immense root systems, acacia and broom are very common. The presence of trees obviously indicates the presence of water and many wadis are densely covered with vegetation even though the wadis themselves appear to be bone dry.

I shall not give a list of the Saharan flora; the distribution is very uneven and many of the species are hard to identify, but you will find many of the Mediterranean species, particularly in the north and in the Hoggar and Tibesti mountain ranges.

The struggle for survival of African flora is made harder by the continual overgrazing of nomadic herds as well as by the indiscriminate removal of 'timber' as fuel. It is the duty of the Saharan traveller to protect and conserve. Use only fallen twigs and branches for fires. Avoid running over isolated tufts of greenery.

13

Climate

The inhabitants of the Sahara have a saying 'The Sahara is a cold place where there is a hot sun.'

The truth of this will often be apparent. It is very difficult for Europeans and Americans, brought up on tales about the scorching heat of the Sahara, to adapt to the idea of actually freezing in the desert. The water holes on the Hoggar in the Central Sahara freeze on most nights during winter.

The main characteristic of the Saharan climate is the dryness of the atmosphere. The relative humidity is so low that in many parts a layer of water—if such there was—fifteen feet thick would evaporate each year. There are side effects to this extraordinary dryness, such as electrostatic phenomena—sparks from clothing, hair standing on end and so on; fingernails become very brittle; humans and animals become dehydrated.

The temperature and rainfall table (Appendix A) gives some idea of conditions. The average annual precipitation is about four inches in the north and six in the south. In the extreme north snow falls exceptionally. The distribution of rain is most uneven and for several consecutive years no rain falls in some areas, but precipitation can be very heavy—three inches in twenty-four hours has been recorded. Such rain, as may be imagined, does devastating damage to the mud houses of the inhabitants.

For most of the winter much of the Sahara is cloudless, but as spring arrives the clouds appear and by late summer cloud

113

may cover the whole of the Southern Sahara. Conversely cloud cover appears in the north during the winter. The middle Sahara is the most cloudless—150 days is the average.

Strangely the highest temperatures are to be found in the Northern Sahara: Ain Salah has the reputation for holding the record but the single highest figure was recorded in Tindouf: 57·1°C (135°F).

The reason for these high temperatures in the north is the south wind, known variously as the *Sirocco*, *Khamsin* or *Irifi*. The wind is most unpleasant and in summer it can blow day after day for about seven hours at a stretch, maintaining a temperature up to 44°C (111°F). In July or August the sand can reach a temperature of 70°C (168°F) during the day.

The prevailing wind blows during the winter between the south west and the north west; during the summer it blows in the opposite direction. Certain areas, such as the Ténéré, experience only a north to east wind. The wind can be a nuisance but it also provides a welcome breeze during periods of great heat. It seldom blows at night.

Sandstorms owe their existence to this wind. They are quite frequent during the spring, varying greatly in intensity but normally blowing only during the day. Some areas experience almost none—others perhaps fifty days or more each year.

Taken at its best the Saharan climate is almost perfect—cool nights, hot (but not too hot), dry days.

Sandstorms

Anyone exposed to the full force of a sandstorm will not readily forget the experience. The onset is often heralded by the arrival of a big black cloud which can completely obscure the sun. This may be apparent the day before the storm arrives. A favourite starting time for sandstorms is eight-thirty in the morning. It may blow hard for a day, less hard for the second and will probably cease on the third day. If not it can blow on for another week! While it is blowing hard it is impossible to move—visibility is reduced to a few yards and to expose yourself to its force is madness; the sand has sufficient power just above ground level to remove stove enamel from metal and in an area of loose sand to bury you in a few minutes.

At the approach of a sandstorm you should position the vehicle on the highest available ground, choosing a site of hard rock or hard sand if possible, and with the back of the vehicle to the storm. Make sure you have all the water and food you need inside the vehicle. Cover your head with a Tuareg-type veil and wear goggles if you have them. The sand will appear to be blowing straight through the vehicle, even if everything is shut and, if it is shut, the temperature will be almost unbearable. A severe storm is an extremely uncomfortable experience.

Water

The water table in the Sahara continues to become lower. A situation already desperate is becoming worse. This will affect you, the desert traveller, in a number of ways; you will encounter nomads begging for water; you will find wells marked on the map which are now dry; you may find people looking askance when you fill half a dozen jerrycans in an oasis. All this means that you should treat water, even though it has cost you nothing, as a precious commodity. When you come to a desert well, tempting though it is to splash it around, you should not waste it; the lives of an entire caravan may depend on there being water in that well. Give all the water you can spare to those who beg for it.

14

Health in the Desert

Because it is clean and empty, the Sahara is essentially a healthy place. The desert traveller, however, will punctuate his journey at numerous inhabited places where certain precautions are desirable.

The first difficulty, even in the desert, can be a straightforward accident requiring first aid, so buy a good first-aid kit and instruction book or better still include an experienced practitioner in the expedition; ensure that this kit is always kept in an accessible place known to all. Accidents can occur; I have even come across a collision between two vehicles on a piece of open desert some one hundred miles or more from any other vehicle! Burns caused by petrol stoves are perhaps a particular hazard and a bottle of pure water for instant application is a worthwhile precaution.

Diseases endemic to the area are also a problem. The obvious way to reduce the risk is by inoculation, vaccination or suitable prophylactic. All the Saharan countries have inoculation and vaccination requirements but since these are subject to change at short notice it is best to check with a travel agent or the respective countries. See also Appendix C.

Whether or not it is compulsory for the visitor, it is basic good sense to guard against endemic diseases and infections. Inoculations or vaccinations should be obtained for smallpox, typhoid, paratyphoid (TAB), tetanus, poliomyelitis and cholera, plus yellow fever for the Southern Sahara only. Some

Page 117 OASES
30 A mud village in the Dogon district, Mali
31 Tamarisks shade the main street in Tamanrasset, Algeria

WATER IN THE DESERT

32 Drawing water at the Achegour well in the Ténéré desert; water from such isolated wells should be most sparingly drawn

33 First bathe after crossing the desert! The pool at the campsite outside Agadés, Niger

Page 119
ROCK PAINTINGS
34 Thousands of paintings
   and engravings exist
   in the Tassili and
   Hoggar mountains;
   thousands more await
   discovery
35 A party sets off to
   climb a Tassili escarp-
   ment at the top of
   which are numerous
   groups of paintings.
   The going is rough.
   steep, long and very
   hot but greatly
   rewarding

recommend an injection of gamma globulin for protection against hepatitis but its efficiency is open to question and its duration is short.

These precautions should be taken in plenty of time—if possible three months before departure. This not only allows a sufficient time interval between those inoculations which need multiple doses (TAB for example) but enables incompatible inoculations to be spread out; such as smallpox and yellow fever, poliomyelitis and yellow fever. Also, some inoculations produce unpleasant effects for a short period.

Malaria has to be taken seriously since it can be a killer. Many people give it scant thought, probably because it is so readily preventable that it has lost its sinister reputation. There are still over 250 million cases of malaria per year. The whole of both the Atlas region and the Southern Sahara are malarially infected. Several types of preventative pills are available. Those which are taken daily, such as Paludrin, are in my view much easier to remember than those which need to be taken only once a week.

By far the most common ailment affecting the Saharan traveller is one of the many forms of 'gippy tummy'. These can range from acute dysentery to a mild upset. They are usually caused by drinking contaminated water, milk or uncooked food, food contaminated by flies, or undercooked food or rewarmed food. The best way to avoid these upsets is to follow the advice given. Streptotriad pills, both as prophylactic and cure, are possibly the best buy.

Water purification is not something to leave to chance. It is easy, when planning an expedition, to assume that one will boil or otherwise disinfect all water. But in the rush of the moment, impelled by a consuming thirst and the prospect of slaking it with crystal-clear, cool water drawn from a clean-looking well, one tends to be less particular! Filtration removes suspended matter from water but does not necessarily purify it completely. The only safe methods are by chemical disinfection or boiling.

Boiling is the best method in theory since it leaves the water completely pure and tasteless. But in the heat of the desert four people can easily drink six gallons a day—to say nothing of water for washing face, hands, teeth, cooking utensils and so on —so the practical problem is considerable. Two types of tablet which purify by chlorination are Halozone and Sterotabs. I recommend these and would advise taking at least twice as many as you calculate you need. They must be used in adequate strength. If the water looks dirty it should be filtered first. Taste-removing tablets are also available.

It cannot be too strongly emphasised that all water should be considered suspect, irrespective of its reputation or appearance. Many people who travel extensively, and many who live in potentially infected areas, seem to have a blind spot about water purity. Only recently I met a resident of obvious good sense whose father had died of bilharzia, a very unpleasant waterborne disease. In spite of numerous precautions taken in other directions he continued to drink unpurified local water.

Tap water, even in first-class hotels, is not safe. Nor is bottled water in unsealed bottles. Some of the Saharan tour companies take inadequate precautions for ensuring that their customers drink only pure water; it can therefore be wise to take your own purifying tablets.

Bilharzia (schistosomiasis) is a parasitical infection passed from the freshwater snail to man. If you bathe or even paddle in such water the larvae of this parasite can penetrate your skin; if you drink such water you are similarly at risk. There are two forms of the disease and one or other is endemic in most Saharan countries.

The last horrific disease worthy of mention is rabies. There is quite a high incidence of this in Africa and if allowed to develop it is always fatal. Rabies is normally contracted from the bite of an infected (rabid) dog. The skin needs to be broken for the transference to occur but the infection can occur from a dog licking an existing scratch or cut. Typically a rabid dog salivates excessively. The wound should be washed (not scrubbed) immediately with large quantities of soapy water (a tap is best). It is then vital to obtain anti-rabietic serum from a hospital as soon as possible. The incubation period is from thirty to sixty days, so provided appropriate treatment is taken as soon as possible, rabies will not develop. But do not try to make a friend of every dog you encounter.

Snakes and scorpions

Out of all proportion to the danger they actually present, snakes and scorpions arouse an unreasoning fear in many travellers, including myself. The thought of a confrontation with a saw-scaled viper or a spitting cobra represents for me a deterrent to Saharan travel which far exceeds the sum total of all other hazards, many of which are infinitely greater! I have found, to my comfort, that this consuming fear is common, particularly amongst men.

Whatever the actual danger, legends launched by imaginative travellers have bestowed upon these creatures a reputation for extraordinary animosity and cunning. Scorpions hiding in shoes waiting for the insertion of a nice juicy toe, snakes slithering under the sand bent on torpedoing your foot; such images send shivers down the spine.

Driven by fear, I have attempted to come to terms with the danger by objective investigation. But my terror has gradually been reduced more by never actually having seen a snake, despite quite a lot of time spent in places reputed to be 'infested'. I have met others, some far more Sahara-travelled than I, who have also never seen snakes or heard of anyone being bitten. However, it is unreasonable to dismiss the danger altogether. In many cases scorpions are quite often seen, especially in summer, and if you hunt around long enough you may either see a snake or hear of a case of snakebite. Fatal bites or stings are definitely rare and usually confined to the very old, young or unfit. However, if you belong to the happy species of intrepid traveller for whom neither snake nor scorpion holds the least terror, let me quickly restore the balance by mentioning the package tour traveller. Last year he was stung severely by a scorpion in a certain oasis towards the beginning of the tour and was forced to miss the rest of the tour. Greatly disappointed but undeterred by his experience, he returned the next year for an identical trip. It is hardly necessary to add that, in the same oasis, and almost in the same spot, he was bitten in the same foot by a highly poisonous snake!

To put it in perspective, it is most unlikely that you will be bitten or that an attack would make you seriously ill. But if this reassurance is not sufficient, it will be a comfort to know that suitable sera are available both for snakebites and scorpion stings. In Appendix D you will find the addresses of sera suppliers, the species covered and the cost. For this to be effective you need the associated equipment of syringe and tourniquet and someone who knows how to use them. It is essential that the instructions be learnt beforehand; there can be serious side-effects and appropriate precautions must be taken. Storing sera can be a problem since it must be protected from light, frost and temperatures above 15°C. (Higher temperatures shorten its life.)

Incidentally, the 'classic' first-aid measures of making incisions near the bite or trying to suck out the venom of the wound are quite useless. If medical attention is available within a short period of time it is preferable to the use of anti-snake venom.

General

Sunburn may sound a mild complaint compared to the fearsome diseases just discussed but it is capable of producing a serious condition. If you go straight from a northern climate and strip off in the desert, soaking up the sun for two or three hours, you will certainly need hospital treatment by the same evening. Even fifteen minutes exposure on a white skin can produce a memorable burn; calamine lotion is probably still the best antidote for mild burns. The solution to sunburn lies in two precautions: minimal exposure initially (perhaps ten minutes, thirty minutes, one hour, two hours on successive days) and either a good brand of suncream or Vitamin A pills such as Sylvasun.

To summarise some of the key points for good health, here are my suggestions:

Have inoculations and vaccinations in good time.

Take comprehensive first-aid kit.

Wear light, loose-fitting clothes containing a minimum of man-made fibres; on no account wear nylon clothing.

Arrange journey schedule which allows plenty of spare time, particularly in early stages.

Drink plenty; approximately 1 pint per 10°F per day; ie in a temperature of 100°F you will need to drink 10 pints.

Take salt tablets.

Do not over-expose to sun at first.

Ensure food and drink are uncontaminated.

Be well covered after dark; in mosquito areas tuck trouser legs into boots.

Do not walk around bare-footed.

Avoid bathing in any water not known to be free of bilharzia.

Shake shoes before putting them on.

If bitten by a dog, go at once to a hospital after first washing the bite.

Have a thorough dental check-up before leaving.

15

Desert Survival

Typical of the useless advice contained in books of this sort are admonitions to the traveller, who is probably several hundred miles from the nearest human being, to 'go at once to a local hospital' or 'catch local game by setting snares'. So that this book is no exception I will open the chapter by saying that, no matter what goes wrong, there should not be a survival problem because in the open desert you should be travelling in convoy. The justification for this section, therefore, lies in the possibility of *all* vehicles being stranded!

In the desert there is only one paramount requirement for survival: water. In these notes I have assumed that rescue will be organised within a reasonable period; in other words, your intended route and schedule will have been made known to someone able to put in hand a rescue operation. It must also be supposed that you have not deviated greatly from your intended route.

The quantity of water you are carrying is likely to determine the time you will survive. On long desert crossings this can lead to interesting equations with petrol and water, as the chances are that you will be tempted to sacrifice water for petrol.

The maximum sustainable water loss in an average adult is twenty pints. In an ambient air temperature of 100°F the water loss, in twenty-four hours, even in a body at rest, is about half this amount. The ambient temperature at night, however, will be much lower and the loss of water substantially less. But energy expenditure in the heat of the sun will cause a loss of at least a pint an hour. A simple calculation shows that each person will need a jerrycan of water for three days' survival without dehydration, under conditions of extreme heat. Under such circumstances the advantages of taking few passengers become wonderfully apparent.

In terms of survival, a considerable margin is provided by the body's ability to consume its own water content. No permanent harm is done to a man who consumes ten per cent of his own weight by dehydration if this loss is subsequently restored. The point of fatality is about twenty-five per cent. Thus with a full jerrycan of water, taking no exercise at all and keeping in the shade all day, with low night temperatures and a daily maximum of 100°F, you might expect to survive twelve days. Under similar conditions, but walking all night until exhausted, six days, and walking by day, three days.

Dehydration is the enemy. At equal temperatures the body requires up to three times as much water to maintain water balance in the desert as it requires in the high humidity of the jungle. Thirst is not a safe indication of how much water you need since you can still dehydrate while satisfying your thirst. Thirst is a sympton of dehydration but so also are slow motion, loss of appetite, nausea, drowsiness and high temperatures.

To conserve water, keep on your clothing, including a hat. This slows the rate of sweat evaporation and helps insulate the body from the heat of the sun. Sit or lie in the shade and raise the body a foot or so from the ground—it can be 30°F hotter on the surface compared to a foot above it. Keep the mouth shut; breath through the nose; avoid conversation. Cover lips with grease. Alchohol accelerates dehydration. Minimise food intake if sufficient water is not available.

The golden rule is to stay with your vehicle. If in the least doubt observe this rule. However, if you are within a few miles of an oasis and you know its direction it is obviously better to walk there than to risk dying of thirst. The distance at which this becomes feasible is a question of physical fitness, terrain and directional certainty. Because of the limit to the amount of water you can carry, it is probably about two days' (or rather nights') walking—perhaps thirty to forty miles. It is useful to carry light-weight collapsible plastic bottles of gallon capacity. It is wise too to carry a survival ration of high calorie dry food bars made of cereal, powdered milk, honey and fruit, though food is less of a problem. In an emergency a human being can survive for weeks on extremely little food. Obviously the food you can eat will be considered for its liquid content and nutrient balance. If foraging for plants avoid eating anything with milky sap and boil plants if possible. Taste before eating; if bitter, nauseating or burning, do not eat.

To find water in the desert is not impossible. A dry looking wadi may have water just below the surface. Look at the lowest point on the outside of a bend in the river channel. Dig until you find wet sand; water may seep out of the sand into the hole. Dig at the base of any slope with green vegetation. Look at the base of rock cliffs. Watch for trails or bird flights converging toward a particular spot. To augment water supplies you should construct a solar still and carry a plastic sheet two yards square for this purpose.

The solar still

Dig a hole in an unshaded spot (preferably in a natural depression or a dry river bed). The hole should be round, three feet in diameter and about two feet to three feet deep. Position collecting bucket in the hole. Lay a six foot by six foot square sheet of polythene over the hole, pile enough sand around the edge to hold it securely and, by placing a small rock on the plastic sheet, form a cone with the point just above the bucket. A pint of water or more should have collected in the bucket in twenty-four hours.

The solar still is operated by the sun's heat raising the temperature of the air and soil under the plastic, thus hastening vaporisation of water from the soil. When the air under the plastic becomes saturated the vapour condenses in tiny drops on the underside of the plastic, the plastic being cooler than the damp air under it. The drops run slowly down the sloping underside of the plastic and drip off into the bucket. Because solar energy provides the heat for the still, it might seem that darkness would halt production. After sundown, however, the plastic cools rapidly, while the temperature of the soil remains high. So water vapour continues to condense on the under-surface of the plastic. You will also probably catch a 'meal' of beetles, ants, etc in the cone overnight.

Move as little as possible. Think before you act. Prevent panic. If you do decide to abandon the vehicle, leave clear instructions indicating your route, supplies carried, time of departure and so on.

Walk slowly, resting ten minutes in the hour. Navigate by the north pole star, but for convenience use a star closer to the horizon, reselecting every ten minutes to compensate for the earth's rotation. Although natural obstacles may cause difficulties during night travel, and you may miss indications of water and habitation, you will be more than compensated by the conservation of energy and water and navigational accuracy. If you decide to travel in daylight, move only in the early morning and late evening. Go round instead of over. Maintain a steady, easy step. When walking in soft sand, lean well forward, keeping the knees bent. Do not swing the arms but grasp your shirt at the shoulder seams. When you rest, remove your shoes and prop your feet up high.

Mark your path if you can, in case you have to retrace your steps. Marks in the sand, bits of paper beneath stones, small stone cairns, pieces of stick and so on will provide a record of your route where footmarks disappear. Sandstorms may remove even these marks, so more permanent landmarks (arrow heads in stones) at the summit of prominent points will help. Travel the ridges rather than the valleys. Use a compass if you have one.

If you are retracing your steps, never take short cuts; it is a quick way to become confused. Do not travel in a sand storm; cover your head with a cloth and sit it out as best you can.

To determine direction using a watch, the watch needs to show correct 'sun-time'. Hold the watch level and point the hour hand at the sun. *South* will be midway (in the smaller angle) between the hour hand and the figure 12.

To determine direction from a shadow without knowing the time, select an object at least three foot high which casts a good sharp shadow. Mark the shadow tip, wait fifteen minutes and mark it again. A line drawn from the first mark through the second will point *east*.

Signalling is an effective method of attracting attention, especially from the air.

REQUIRE DOCTOR SERIOUS INJURIES	I	PROBABLY SAFE TO LAND HERE	△
REQUIRE MEDICAL SUPPLIES	II	ALL WELL	LL
UNABLE TO PROCEED	X	REQUIRE FUEL AND OIL	L
REQUIRE FOOD AND WATER	F	NO	N
REQUIRE FIREARMS AND AMMUNITION	≫	YES	Y
INDICATE DIRECTION TO PROCEED	K	NOT UNDERSTOOD	⅃L
AM PROCEEDING IN THIS DIRECTION	↑	REQUIRE ENGINEER	W
IF IN DOUBT, USE INTERNATIONAL SYMBOL	SOS	REQUIRE MAP AND COMPASS	□

1. Lay out these symbols by using strips of fabric, pieces of wood, stones or any other available material.

2.   Endeavour to provide as big a colour contrast as possible between the material used for the symbols and the background against which the symbols are exposed.
3.   Symbols should be at least eight feet in height, and larger if possible. Take care to lay out the symbols exactly as depicted to avoid confusion with other symbols.
4.   In addition to using these symbols, make every effort to attract attention by means of flares, smoke or other available means.
5.   In sand, signals can be made by shovelling channels in the sand.
6.   Pilots should acknowledge message by rocking wings from side to side.

You can also signal with flares (black smoke for day use—rubber tyres are highly effective), fires, torches or headlights, mirrors or whistles. Orange-coloured toy balloons can be filled with lighter-than-air gas from an appropriate aerosol can. Such balloons tethered on as much string as they will lift can be seen from a great distance. Glass removed from the vehicle can be set up on a nearby summit to provide all-round reflection.

It is not normally practical to carry radio equipment. One reason for this is the suspicion felt by national customs officers for any signal transmitting equipment.

However, if MF/HF survival radio is carried, it should be set up as soon as possible and be operated for a period of four minutes, at approximately ten-minute intervals. When an accurate watch is available, transmissions on 500 kc/s should be made during the international silence periods of three minutes, starting at H+15 and H+45. Similarly transmissions on 2182 kc/s should be made during the international silence periods of three minutes, starting at H and H+30.

Quicksand

Quicksand is a deposit of fine sand in combination with

water. It may have the appearance of smooth dry sand, but the water underneath lubricates the grains and allows them to flow easily. There is nothing mysterious about quicksand—it acts as any thick liquid would, and if we react sensibly we can escape it. Man is lighter and will float in water and, therefore, quicksand. It has no power to suck down bodies, though frantic struggling to free the feet creates forceful downward movement which causes the sand first to move away, then quickly return to pack around the legs. The result is a firmer and deeper hold on the body. Further struggling repeats the process until the body is engulfed completely.

If caught, throw yourself flat on your back. You will float. Get rid of extra weight. Throw away anything you are carrying. Do not hold up your arms but let them rest spread out on the surface. Roll slowly to firm ground, or turn on to your stomach and do a slow breaststroke. Move slowly and carefully and you will 'swim' to safety. But avoid getting caught; look for quicksand in river beds, washes and run-off areas of recent flash floods.

Appendices

APPENDIX A: AVERAGE TEMPERATURE RANGES AND AVERAGE RAINFALL GUIDE

Scale:	F	32	50	68	86	104	122	140	158	176	194	212
	C	0	10	20	30	40	50	60	70	80	90	100

Rainfall: A = 0–2 inches
B = 2–4 inches
C = 4–8 inches
D = 8–12 inches
E = 12–16 inches
F = over 16 inches

Temperatures are shown in Centigrade

TOWN	JAN	FEB	MAR	APR	MAY	JUNE	JULY	AUG	SEPT	OCT	NOV	DEC
London	2–6	2–7	2–9	4–13	7–17	11–20	12–22	12–21	9–18	7–13	4–9	2–7
	A	A	A	A	A	A	B	B	A	B	B	B
Paris	1–6	1–8	3–11	6–15	9–19	12–23	14–25	14–24	11–21	7–15	4–10	1–6
	A	A	A	A	B	B	B	B	A	B	B	B
Abeche	15–38	17–39	21–42	23–44	24–42	24–41	21–36	20–34	20–37	20–40	19–39	15–36
	A	A	A	A	A	A	C	D	B	A	A	A
Accra	23–33	23–33	23–33	23–33	23–33	22–32	21–30	21–28	22–29	22–31	23–32	23–32
	A	A	B	B	C	C	A	A	A	B	A	A
Agadés	10–29	13–33	17–38	21–41	25–44	24–43	24–41	23–38	23–40	20–39	15–35	12–32
	A	A	A	A	A	A	A	B	A	A	A	A
Agadir	7–20	9–22	11–23	13–24	15–24	17–25	18–26	18–27	17–27	15–26	12–24	8–21
	A	A	A	A	A	A	A	A	A	A	A	A

Algiers	9–15 C	10–16 B	11–18 B	13–20 A	15–23 A	18–26 A	21–29 A	22–29 A	20–27 A	17–23 B	13–19 C	10–16 C
Bamako	17–33 A	20–36 A	24–39 A	26–39 A	26–39 B	27–35 C	23–31 D	23–30 E	22–32 D	22–34 B	19–35 A	18–33 A
Bechar	2–16 A	4–19 A	9–22 A	13–27 A	17–31 A	22–36 A	26–40 A	25–39 A	20–34 A	14–27 B	8–20 A	3–16 A
Benghazi	6–21 B	6–23 A	7–30 A	9–34 A	12–38 A	16–38 A	18–34 A	19–33 A	17–36 A	14–33 A	11–29 A	7–24 B
Bilma	6–26 A	8–29 A	13–35 A	17–40 A	21–43 A	22–44 A	23–42 A	24–40 A	21–41 A	16–39 A	11–33 A	8–28 B
Biskra	6–16 A	8–18 A	11–22 A	14–26 A	19–31 A	24–36 A	27–40 A	26–39 A	23–35 A	17–28 A	12–21 A	7–17 A
Casablanca	7–17 B	8–18 A	9–20 A	11–21 A	13–22 A	16–24 A	18–27 A	19–27 A	17–27 A	15–25 A	11–21 B	9–18 B
Conakry	22–31 A	22–31 A	23–32 A	24–32 A	24–31 C	23–29 F	22–28 F	23–27 F	22–29 F	22–30 E	23–31 B	23–31 A
Dakar	18–24 A	17–23 A	17–24 A	19–25 A	20–26 A	23–29 A	25–30 C	25–30 D	24–30 C	25–30 B	23–29 A	20–27 A
Djanet	6–19 A	9–22 A	13–26 A	18–31 A	23–35 A	25–38 A	25–37 A	25–36 A	23–35 A	19–31 A	13–26 A	8–20 A
El Goléa	3–17 A	5–20 A	9–24 A	14–29 A	18–33 A	24–39 A	26–42 A	26–41 A	22–37 A	16–30 A	9–23 A	4–18 A
Faya-Largeau	13–28 A	15–31 A	18–35 A	19–40 A	25–44 A	26–43 A	25–42 A	23–37 A	22–37 A	22–38 A	18–32 A	13–28 A
F'Derick	11–25 A	13–27 A	15–30 A	17–33 A	19–35 A	22–39 A	24–42 A	25–42 A	24–39 A	21–35 A	17–30 A	13–25 A

Average Temperature Ranges and Average Rainfall Guide—continued

TOWN	JAN	FEB	MAR	APR	MAY	JUNE	JULY	AUG	SEPT	OCT	NOV	DEC
Fort-Lamy	14-34	16-36	20-39	23-41	25-40	24-38	23-34	22-31	22-30	22-37	18-37	15-34
	A	A	A	A	A	B	C	D	B	A	A	A
Gao	14-30	18-33	21-37	25-40	28-43	27-41	25-38	24-35	24-38	22-39	20-37	16-32
	A	A	A	A	A	A	B	C	A	A	A	A
Ghadames	3-18	4-21	8-26	12-31	18-36	22-41	23-42	22-41	19-38	15-32	9-25	5-19
	A	A	A	A	A	A	A	A	A	A	A	A
Hon	2-20	4-22	7-26	10-31	15-34	19-38	18-39	19-39	18-37	14-32	9-26	4-21
	A	A	A	A	A	A	A	A	A	A	A	A
Kano	9-36	11-38	14-41	19-42	21-41	19-38	19-34	18-33	19-34	16-35	13-37	11-35
	A	A	A	A	B	C	D	E	C	A	A	A
Kayes	12-38	15-42	18-45	21-46	22-46	20-43	19-38	20-35	20-37	19-39	16-40	13-39
	A	A	A	A	B	B	C	D	C	A	A	A
Kufra	7-21	8-24	12-28	17-32	21-39	23-39	24-38	24-38	21-35	18-32	14-28	9-22
	A	A	A	A	A	A	A	A	A	A	A	A
Laghouat	2-13	4-15	7-18	9-23	13-26	18-32	21-36	20-35	17-30	12-24	6-17	3-13
	A	A	A	A	A	A	A	A	A	A	A	A
Lagos	20-33	22-33	22-34	22-34	22-33	22-31	22-30	21-30	22-31	21-31	22-33	21-33
	A	A	C	C	D	F	D	B	C	D	B	A
Linguere	14-34	16-36	17-39	20-41	21-42	23-40	23-36	23-34	23-34	22-37	18-37	15-34
	A	A	A	A	A	A	C	D	C	A	A	A
Marrakesh	5-19	6-21	9-23	11-26	14-29	17-33	19-38	20-38	18-32	14-29	10-23	6-19
	A	A	A	A	A	A	A	A	A	A	A	A

Murzuk	4–19 A	5–23 A	9–28 A	13–33 A	17–38 A	21–42 A	21–42 A	21–41 A	19–39 A	14–34 A	9–26 A	4–20 A
Niamey	16–34 A	18–36 A	22–39 A	26–41 A	27–41 A	25–38 B	24–34 C	22–32 D	23–34 C	23–36 A	19–37 A	15–34 A
Nouadhibou	13–25 A	13–26 A	14–26 A	15–26 A	16–26 A	17–28 B	19–27 C	20–29 D	20–31 A	19–30 A	17–27 A	15–25 A
Ouargla	4–18 A	6–21 A	10–25 A	14–30 A	18–34 A	23–40 A	25–43 A	25–42 A	22–38 A	16–31 A	10–24 A	6–18 A
Reggane	8–22 A	11–25 A	15–29 A	19–34 A	23–38 A	28–43 A	30–45 A	31–45 A	28–41 A	22–35 A	15–28 A	8–21 A
Sebha	5–19 A	8–22 A	11–26 A	15–31 A	20–36 A	23–39 A	23–38 A	23–39 A	22–37 A	18–33 A	12–26 A	7–21 A
Sfax	7–16 A	8–17 A	10–19 A	12–21 A	15–24 A	19–28 A	21–30 A	22–31 A	21–29 A	18–26 A	12–22 A	8–18 A
Tamanrasset	4–19 A	5–22 A	9–26 A	13–30 A	17–33 A	21–35 A	21–35 A	21–34 A	19–33 A	15–30 A	10–25 A	6–21 A
Tanger	4–19 C	5–22 C	9–26 C	13–30 B	17–33 A	21–35 A	21–35 A	21–34 A	19–33 A	15–30 C	10–25 C	6–21 C
Tidjikda	11–27 A	13–30 A	16–34 A	19–37 A	23–40 A	25–41 A	25–39 A	23–37 B	24–38 A	22–37 A	17–33 A	12–28 A
Timbuktu	13–31 A	15–34 A	19–38 A	22–41 A	26–43 A	27–42 A	25–38 B	24–34 C	24–38 A	24–40 A	18–38 A	14–32 A
Tindouf	6–22 A	7–25 A	12–28 A	14–32 A	16–35 A	19–39 A	25–45 A	25–43 A	22–38 A	16–32 A	12–27 A	7–22 A
Tobruck	6–22 A	5–24 A	7–30 A	9–37 A	12–37 A	16–37 A	19–32 A	19–32 A	18–34 A	14–33 A	11–29 A	7–23 A

Average Temperature Ranges and Average Rainfall Guide—continued

TOWN	JAN	FEB	MAR	APR	MAY	JUNE	JULY	AUG	SEPT	OCT	NOV	DEC
Tripoli	4-21	6-23	7-29	9-35	12-36	15-39	18-37	19-36	18-37	14-34	9-29	6-23
	B	A	A	A	A	A	A	A	A	A	B	B
Tunis	7-15	8-16	9-18	11-21	14-24	18-29	20-32	21-32	20-29	16-25	11-20	8-16
	B	A	A	A	A	A	A	A	A	A	A	B
Zaouia el Kahla	3-19	6-23	10-27	15-32	20-37	25-41	25-43	25-42	23-39	17-33	10-26	5-20
	A	A	A	A	A	A	A	A	A	A	A	A

APPENDIX B: CONVERSION TABLES

metres—feet

m	0	1	2	3	4	5	6	7	8	9	
—	—	3·3	6·6	9·8	13·1	16·4	19·7	23·0	26·2	29·5	10
10	32·8	36·1	39·4	42·6	45·9	49·2	52·2	55·8	59·0	62·3	20
20	65·6	68·9	72·2	75·4	78·7	82·0	85·3	88·6	91·9	95·1	30
30	98·4	101·7	105·0	108·3	111·5	114·8	118·1	121·4	124·7	127·9	40
40	131·2	134·5	137·8	141·1	144·4	147·6	150·9	154·2	157·5	160·8	50
50	164·0	167·3	170·6	173·9	177·2	180·4	183·7	187·0	190·3	193·6	

feet—metres

ft	0	1	2	3	4	5	6	7	8	9	
—	—	0·3	0·6	0·9	1·2	1·5	1·8	2·1	2·4	2·7	—
10	3·0	3·4	3·7	4·0	4·3	4·6	4·9	5·2	5·5	5·8	10
20	6·1	6·4	6·7	7·0	7·3	7·6	7·9	8·2	8·5	8·8	20
30	9·1	9·4	9·7	10·1	10·4	10·7	11·0	11·3	11·6	11·9	30
40	12·2	12·5	12·8	13·1	13·4	13·7	14·0	14·3	14·6	14·9	40
50	15·2	15·5	15·8	16·2	16·5	16·8	17·1	17·4	17·7	18·0	50

kilometres—miles

km	0	1	2	3	4	5	6	7	8	9	
—	—	0·6	1·2	1·9	2·5	3·1	3·7	4·3	5·0	5·6	—
10	6·2	6·8	7·5	8·1	8·7	9·3	9·9	10·6	11·2	11·8	10
20	12·4	13·0	13·7	14·3	14·9	15·5	16·2	16·8	17·4	18·0	20
30	18·6	19·3	19·9	20·5	21·1	21·7	22·4	23·0	23·6	24·2	30

Conversion Tables—continued

kilometres—miles

km	0	1	2	3	4	5	6	7	8	9
40	24.9	25.5	26.1	26.7	27.3	28.0	28.6	29.2	29.8	30.4
50	31.1	31.7	32.3	32.9	33.6	34.2	34.8	35.4	36.0	36.7
60	37.3	37.9	38.5	39.1	39.8	40.4	41.0	41.6	42.2	42.9
70	43.5	44.1	44.7	45.4	46.0	46.6	47.2	47.8	48.5	49.1
80	49.7	50.3	50.9	51.6	52.2	52.8	53.4	54.1	54.7	55.3
90	55.9	56.5	57.2	57.8	58.4	59.0	59.7	60.3	60.9	61.5

miles—kilometres

miles	0	1	2	3	4	5	6	7	8	9
—		1.6	3.2	4.8	6.4	8.0	9.7	11.3	12.9	14.5
10	16.1	17.7	19.3	20.9	22.5	24.1	25.8	27.4	29.0	30.6
20	32.2	33.8	35.4	37.0	38.6	40.2	41.8	43.5	45.1	46.7
30	48.3	49.9	51.5	53.1	54.7	56.3	57.9	59.5	61.2	62.8
40	64.4	66.0	67.6	69.2	70.8	72.4	74.0	75.6	77.2	78.9
50	80.5	82.1	83.7	85.3	86.9	88.5	90.1	91.7	93.3	95.0
60	96.6	98.2	99.8	101.4	103.0	104.6	106.2	107.8	109.4	111.0
70	112.7	114.3	115.9	117.5	119.1	120.7	122.3	123.9	125.5	127.1
80	128.7	130.4	132.0	133.6	135.2	136.8	138.4	140.0	141.6	143.2
90	144.8	146.5	148.1	149.7	151.3	152.9	154.5	156.1	157.7	159.3

miles per gallon—kilometres per gallon

mpg	kpg	mpg	kpg	mpg	kpg	mpg	kpg	mpg	kpg
12	19.3	20	32.2	28	45.1	36	57.9	50	80.5
14	22.5	22	35.4	30	48.3	38	61.2	55	88.5
16	25.8	24	38.6	32	51.5	40	64.4	60	96.6
18	29.0	26	41.8	34	54.7	45	72.4		

litres—imperial gallons

litres	0	1	2	3	4	5	6	7	8	9	
—	—	0·2	0·4	0·7	0·9	1·1	1·3	1·5	1·8	2·0	—
10	2·2	2·4	2·6	2·9	3·1	3·3	3·5	3·7	4·0	4·2	10
20	4·4	4·6	4·8	5·1	5·3	5·5	5·7	5·9	6·2	6·4	20
30	6·6	6·8	7·0	7·3	7·5	7·7	7·9	8·1	8·4	8·6	30
40	8·8	9·0	9·2	9·5	9·7	9·9	10·1	10·3	10·6	10·8	40
50	11·0	11·2	11·4	11·7	11·9	12·1	12·3	12·5	12·8	13·0	50

imperial gallons—litres

galls	0	1	2	3	4	5	6	7	8	9	
—	—	4·5	9·1	13·6	18·2	22·7	27·3	31·8	36·4	40·9	—
10	45·5	50·0	54·6	59·1	63·6	68·2	72·7	77·3	81·8	86·4	10

pounds per square inch—kilograms per square centimetre

psi	0	1	2	3	4	5	6	7	8	9	
—	—	0·07	0·14	0·21	0·28	0·35	0·42	0·49	0·56	0·63	—
10	0·70	0·77	0·84	0·91	0·98	1·06	1·13	1·20	1·27	1·34	10
20	1·41	1·48	1·55	1·62	1·69	1·76	1·83	1·90	1·97	2·04	20
30	2·11	2·18	2·25	2·32	2·39	2·46	2·53	2·60	2·67	2·74	30

kilograms per square centimetre—pounds per square inch

	0	1	2	3	4	5	6	7	8	9	
—	—	14·2	28·4	42·7	56·9	71·1	85·3	99·6	113·8	128·0	—
10	142·2	156·5	170·7	184·9	199·1	213·4	227·6	241·8	256·0	270·2	10
20	284·5	298·7	312·9	327·1	341·4	355·6	369·8	384·0	398·3	412·5	20
30	426·7	440·9	455·2	469·4	483·6	497·8	512·0	526·3	540·5	554·7	30

Conversion Tables—continued

kilograms—pounds

kg	0	1	2	3	4	5	6	7	8	9	
—	—	2·2	4·4	6·6	8·8	11·0	13·2	15·4	17·6	19·8	—
10	22·0	24·3	26·5	28·7	30·9	33·1	35·3	37·5	39·7	41·9	**10**
20	44·1	46·3	48·5	50·7	52·9	55·1	57·3	59·5	61·7	63·9	**20**
30	66·1	68·3	70·5	72·7	74·9	77·2	79·4	81·6	83·8	86·0	**30**
40	88·2	90·4	92·6	94·8	97·0	99·2	101·4	103·6	105·8	108·0	**40**
50	110·2	112·4	114·6	116·8	119·0	121·3	123·5	125·7	127·9	130·1	**50**

pounds—kilograms

lb	0	1	2	3	4	5	6	7	8	9	
—	—	0·5	0·9	1·4	1·8	2·3	2·7	3·2	3·6	4·1	—
10	4·5	5·0	5·4	5·9	6·4	6·8	7·3	7·7	8·2	8·6	**10**
20	9·1	9·5	10·0	10·4	10·9	11·3	11·8	12·2	12·7	13·2	**20**
30	13·6	14·1	14·5	15·0	15·4	15·9	16·3	16·8	17·2	17·7	**30**
40	18·1	18·6	19·1	19·5	20·0	20·4	20·9	21·3	21·8	22·2	**40**
50	22·7	23·1	23·6	24·0	24·5	24·9	25·4	25·9	26·3	26·8	**50**

Appendix C

Algeria

Main towns

Algiers (1,200,000) capital, Oran (325,000), Constantine (255,000).

Climate

Coastal temperatures range from 13°C–24°C but the Sahara itself reaches 43°C during the day. The *Sirocco* blows hot from the south.

Public Holidays

1 January, 1 May, 19 June, 5 July, 1 November.
Moslem holidays: Aid el Adha, Moslem New Year, Achoura, Moulod, Aid el Fitr. British Embassy also observes British holidays.

Hours of Business

Saturday and Sunday are official holidays. Summer: 1 July to 30 September.
Businesses and Government Offices:

> Winter: 08.00 to 12.00 and 15.00 to 18.00 Monday to Friday.
> Summer: 08. 00 to 13.00 and 15.00 to 18.00 Monday and
> Thursday.
> 08.00 to 13.00 Tuesday, Wednesday, Friday.

Banks: 07.45 to 11.15 and 14.00 to 16.00 Monday to Friday.
British Embassy 08.30 to 12.30 and 14.30 to 17.30 Monday to Friday.
(emergency service) 08.30 to 12.00 Saturday morning.

Currency

Algerian dinar (DA) is divided into 100 centimes.

Any amount of foreign currency may be taken into Algeria. However, there is a limit of DA 50 in Algerian bank notes. It is necessary to obtain a certificate from the customs showing what currency is taken into the country; this certificate must be produced and duly endorsed whenever foreign currency is exchanged for Algerian currency in Algeria and produced when leaving Algeria.

Illegal to reconvert Algerian dinars into foreign currency and changing money presents problems for much of the time. The Bureaux de Change at airports will not always accept travellers' cheques and will sometimes only change foreign bank notes. The Banque Nationale d'Algérie is the only institution officially authorised to change travellers' cheques. The Hotel Aletti in Algiers will accept travellers' cheques in payment of bills, as will the Hotel St George and the town office of Air Algérie, sometimes. Visitors can obtain sea, air or rail tickets when leaving Algeria only with foreign currency.

Appendix C

Electricity
Single phase 127 volts or 3-phase 127/220/330 AC, 50 cycles. Hotels have both 127 and 220 volts. Lamp fittings are both bayonet and screw.

Customs
Free of duty: 200 cigarettes or 50 cigars or 14 ounces of tobacco; bottle of spirits and 2 bottles of wine.

General
Population: 14·3 million. 70 per cent live by agriculture.
British Embassy: Résidence Cassiopée,
Batiment B,
7 Chemin de Glycines,
Algiers. Telephone 60.56.01-04.
Algeria became a Republic in 1962, having been a French territory. Official language is Arabic, although much French is spoken.
Religion: Moslem; alcohol is forbidden to Moslems, though not to Algerians.
Cereals, citrus fruits and vegetables grown mostly in the north. Major wealth is derived from oil wells. Country becoming industrialised with some speed.

Chad

Main town
Fort Lamy (150,000) capital.

Climate
In north, ranges from 48°C during day to freezing at night. Average annual temperature: 28°C.

Public Holidays
1, 11 January; 2 April; 1, 25 May; 11 August; 1, 28 November; 25 December. Moslem holidays (see Algeria); Easter Monday, Whit Monday.

Hours of Business
See Niger.

Currency
CFA franc.

General
Population: 3,600,000. 96 per cent rural nomadic. 1,350,000 employed.
British Embassy: Whitehall, London (telephone 01-930 2323).
Became an independent Republic in 1960: formerly French Equatorial Africa.

Religion: Moslem.

95% of the population are illiterate; 3 out of 10 children attend school.

One of the least economically developed countries in Africa and desperately poor. Receives economic aid from France. Income per head: about CFA francs 5,000 (£8) pa in late 1960s. Most people raise cattle. Sorghum, millet, rice, beans, cassava beans, cotton, dates, peanuts, wheat, tropical fruit grown. Only exports are natron (washing soda) and tungsten. Livestock raised but limited by tsetse fly, especially in south. 300,000 camels, 4,000,000 cattle, 5,000,000 sheep and goats. No railways, 12,000km of roads. River transportation most important.

Libya

Divided into three sections: Tripolitania (west), Cyrenaica (east), Fezzan (south).

Main towns
Tripoli (380,000) capital, Benghazi (321,000).

Climate
4°C–45°C. *Ghibli,* dry wind from the south in June, July and August.

Electricity
125 volts, 50 cycles AC in Tripolitania; 220 volts, 50 cycles AC in Benghazi. Plugs are 2-pin round; lamp fittings: screw.

Public Holidays
28 March, 11 June, 23 July, 1 September, 7 October. Moslem holidays (see Algeria). British Embassy also observes Christian holidays.

Hours of Business
Friday is the official holiday. Summer: 1 April to 31 October.

Government Offices:	Winter: 08.00 to 14.00 Saturday to Thursday.	
	Summer: 07.00 to 13.00 Saturday to Thursday.	
Banks:	Winter: 09.00 to 13.00.	
	Summer: 08.00 to 12.00 Monday, Tuesday, Thursday, Sunday.	
	15.30 to 17.30 Saturday, Wednesday.	
Businesses:	Winter: 08.30 to 12.30 and 15.00 to 17.30.	
	Summer: 08.00 to 12.00 and 14.30 to 17.00.	
British Embassy:	08.30 to 10.00 and 12.30 to 14.00.	
	Monday to Saturday.	

Currency
Libyan dinar, divided into 1,000 dirhams.
Limit of 20 Libyan dinars in bank notes may be taken in or out of Libya.

No limit on other currencies, credit notes or travellers' cheques, but all must be declared and amount taken out not exceed amount taken in. The form filled in on entry must not be lost—required on departure.

Customs
Limit of 200 cigarettes, ½kg tobacco, ¼l perfume into Libya free of duty. Absolutely no alcohol may be taken into country, nor drugs.

General
Population: 1·8 million (1968), mostly living in Tripolitania.
British Embassy: 30 Tariq al Fatah,
                   Tripoli.
                   Telephone: 31191
Official language: Arabic. (Some Italian spoken).
Time: 2 hours ahead of GMT.
Efforts to prevent drift from agriculture to oilfields and towns. Barley, olives, citrus fruit, almonds, tomatoes, tobacco, dates and groundnuts grown.
100,000 private cars.

Mali
Main town
Bamako (130,000) capital.

Climate
Annual average temperature: 30°C in south.

Public Holidays
20 January, 1 May, 25 December. Moslem holidays (see Algeria).

Hours of Business
See Niger.

Currency
Malian franc. No limit to amount of Malian or foreign currency brought into Mali but this must be declared. Remember to exchange Malian currency before leaving country.

General
Population: 5,021,000 (1970) of which 90 per cent is rural.
British Embassy: 20 rue du Docteur Guillet,
                 BP 6025,
                 Dakar, Senegal.
                 Telephone: 22383.

Republic. French (called the French Sudan) until 1958.

Religion: Moslem, some Animists (who believe that all objects have souls).

95 per cent of the population is illiterate. Only 10 per cent of the children attend school.

Chief products: cotton, livestock, millet, peanuts, rice, shea nuts, sorghum. Gold, iron, salt.

Economy: Mali receives aid from France, USA and Communist China. 7 million goats and sheep, 3½ million cattle, plus camels, donkeys, horses. 8,000 miles of road but many impassable during rainy season.

Mauritania

Main town
Nouakchott (45,000) new capital.

Climate
Dry season December to May.

Electricity
127 volts for lighting, 220 volts for power, 50 cycles AC. Plugs and sockets are round 2-pin type. Lamp holders screw-type.

Public Holidays
See Algeria for Moslem holidays. All Sundays.

Business Hours
Businesses: 08.00/09.00 to 12.00 and 15.00 to 18.00 Monday to Friday.
08.00/09.00 to 12.00 Saturday.

Shops: 08.00 to 12.00 and 14.30 to 18.00 Monday to Saturday. (Shop opening hours vary; some shops are open Sunday morning and closed Monday morning).

Banks: 08.00 to 11.15 and 14.30 to 16.30 Monday to Friday.

Government Offices:
08.00 to 12.00 and 14.30 to 18.00 Monday to Friday.
(Some may close between 11.00 and 15.00 on Friday).

British Embassy:
November to June: 08.30 to 12.45 and 15.00 to 18.00 Monday to Friday.
July to October: 08.00 to 13.00 Monday to Saturday.

Currency
CFA francs.
Limit of 25,000 CFA francs may be taken in or out of Mauritania. Travellers' cheques cashable if made negotiable in Mauritania.

Customs
No special restrictions.

General
Population: 1½ million (1969). 75 per cent rural nomads. 17,000 wage earners: income about £70 pa per head. Religion: Moslem.
British Embassy: Honorary British Consul,
British Consulate,
Somima, BP 275,
Nouakchott.
Telephone: 23-37.
or the British Embassy in Senegal (see Mali).
French territory until 1960. Financially solvent, but receives aid from France and the EEC.
Chief industries are iron ore and copper.
Only 96km of the 6,186km of road are tarred. 8,000 vehicles in country.
Efforts to improve the small amount of arable farming, in the settled north of the River Senegal, are strong. Gum arabic, millet, maize and dates are grown, with some rice. Large animal population: 500,000 camels, 10,000,000 sheep and goats.

Greenwich Mean Time used.

Morocco
Main towns
Rabat (375,000) capital and seat of Moroccan government, Casablanca (1,500,000), Marrakesh (333,000).

Climate
Coast much cooler (maximum 22°C) than interior where summer maximum is 38°C.

Electricity
50 cycles AC throughout Morocco. Voltages in different towns are: Casablanca, Tangier: 110v, being replaced by 127v. Some 220v; Rabat: 110v, being replaced by 127v; Marrakesh: 115v; Fez: 110v. Bayonet type light fittings and round 2-pin plugs used.

Public Holidays
See Algeria for Moslem holidays.
British Consulate also observes Good Friday, Easter Monday, Whit Monday, Queen's Birthday, August Bank Holiday, Christmas Day, Boxing Day, Sundays.

Appendix C

Hours of Business
Summer: June to September.
Government departments:
    Winter: 08.30 to 12.00, 14.30 to 18.00 Monday to Friday.
                 08.00 to 13.00 Saturday.
    Summer: 08.30 to 12.00, 16.00 to 19.00 Monday to Friday.
                 08.00 to 13.00 Saturday.
Businesses, shops and offices:
    Tangier: 09.00 to 12.00, 16.00 to 20.00.
    Remainder: 09.00 to 12.00, 15.00 to 18.00 or 19.00.
Banks:
    Winter: 08.15 to 11.30, 14.15 to 16.30 Monday to Friday.
    Summer: 08.30 to 11.30, 15.00 to 17.00 Monday to Friday.
British Consulates:
Casablanca: Winter: 08.30 to 12.30, 14.00 to 17.30 Monday to Friday.
            Summer: 08.30 to 13.00 Monday to Friday. 15.15 to 17.15
                            Thursday.
Tangier: Winter: 09.00 to 12.00, 16.00 to 18.00 Monday to Friday.
                     09.00 to 12.00 Saturday.
            Summer: 08.30 to 13.30 Monday to Saturday.

Currency
Dirham (DH) which is divided into 100 centimes.
No Moroccan currency whatever may be taken in or out of Morocco. The amount of foreign currency taken out may not be more than the amount taken in, but no written declaration necessary. To re-exchange foreign currency bought in Morocco, production of bank vouchers relating to the purchase must be produced.

Customs
Free of duty: 400g tobacco, 200 cigarettes or 50 cigars, camera, binoculars, portable radio receiver. One item per person.

General
Population: 15.5 million. 70 per cent agriculture.
British Representatives:
HM Consul-General,   HM Consul-General,
British Consulate-General,   British Consulate General,
60, Boulevard d'Anfa,   52, rue d'Angleterre,
Casablanca. Telephone: 614.40/1   Tangier. Telephone: 158 95/7
Spanish Protectorate in the north and French Protectorate in the south for 44 years until 1956, when Morocco regained its sovereign independence.

Northern coastal ports of Ceuta and Melilla have remained Spanish. King Hussan II acceded to the throne in March, 1961.

Religion: mainly Moslem.

Official language: Moroccan Arabic. Written: Classical Arabic.

Little English spoken.

Food is eaten with fingers of the right hand and a little must be taken of each course at traditional Moroccan meals.

Greenwich Mean Time used.

Despite fertile soil, varied and healthy climate and large amounts of phosphates, the population is poor. Annual income per head: £60. Principal crops: cereals, citrus fruit and vegetables.

Niger

Main towns
Niamey (72,000) capital.

Climate
16°C–41°C. Tornadoes in the south in August. November to January have *Harmattan,* the cool wind.

Electricity
220/380 volts, 50 cycles AC. Plugs are 2-pin round. Lamp fittings: bayonet.

Public Holidays
See Algeria for Moslem holidays.
Christians observe Holy Days, British Bank Holidays and 1 May.

Business Hours
Businesses: 08.00 to 12.00 and 15.00 to 18.30 Monday to Saturday.
Government Offices:
            08.00 to 12.00 and 15.00 to 18.30 Monday to Friday.
            08.00 to 12.00 Saturday.
Banks: 08.00 to 12.00 Monday to Friday.
There is no British Embassy in Niger.

Currency
CFA francs.
No limit to the amount taken into Niger but limit of 125,000 CFA francs may be taken out. Travellers' cheques cashable and foreign currency exchangeable.

Customs
No special restrictions.

General

Population: 4 million (1970). 95 per cent engaged in agriculture.

Per capita income: £30 pa.

Religion: Moslem; some Animists and Christians.

Official language: French.

Almost whole country is desert. Niger receives aid from France, European Development Fund and Canada. Has a heavy trade deficit.

Tap water unsafe to drink.

Roads mainly laterite—10,000 cars, 5,000 commercial vehicles.

River Niger navigable from October to March from Niamey to Gaya.

Ground nuts are main export. Principal crops: millet, sorghum, groundnuts, manioc, niébé, sugar cane. Cotton, rice, onions, maize, potatoes and tobacco grown. 4 million cattle, 6 million goats, 2·3 million sheep, 360,000 camels, 170,000 horses and 360,000 asses.

Time is one hour ahead of Greenwich Mean Time.

Spanish Sahara

Main town

El Aaiun (5,251 in 1960) capital.

Climate

Interior daily range of temperature from 11°C to 44°C but the coast is more temperate.

Official Public Holidays

See Algeria for Moslem holidays. Also Spanish public holidays observed.

General

Estimated population: 48,607 (1966) including 5,500 Europeans. However, between 25,000 and 60,000 people migrate yearly between the Spanish Sahara and Mauritania, so no accurate records are possible.

British Embassy: none. Use: British Consulate,
PO Box 2020,
Las Palmas, Canary Islands.

The religion is Moslem, the population mostly consisting of Arabs and Berbers. The minerals of potash, iron ore and phosphate are undeveloped due to lack of water and lack of roads. Only 'motorised tracks' found.

Camels, goats and sheep are reared and dried fish a main industry.

Tunisia

Main towns

Tunis (800,000) capital, Sfax (250,000), Sousse (150,000), Kairouan (48,000) is Islamic holy place.

Appendix C

Electricity
Mainly 110v: domestic; 220v, 50 cycles AC: industry. Plug fittings are
2-pin square. Lamp fittings: bayonet.

Public Holidays
See Algeria for Moslem holidays.

Business Hours
Summer: 1 July to 15 September.

Businesses:	Winter:	08.00 to 12.00 and 14.00 to 18.00 Monday to Saturday.
	Summer:	07.00 to 14.00 Monday to Saturday.

Government offices:

	Winter:	08.00 to 12.00 and 14.30 to 18.30 Monday to Thursday.
		08.00 to 14.00 Friday.
	Summer:	07.00 to 13.00 Monday to Saturday.
Banks:	Winter:	08.30 to 11.00 and 14.00 to 16.00 Monday to Friday.
Shops:	Winter:	07.30 to 12.00 and 15.00 to 18.00 Monday to Friday.
	Summer:	07.30 to 12.00 and 16.00 to 18.30 Monday to Friday.

British Embassy:

	Winter:	08.00 to 13.00 and 14.30 to 17.00 Monday to Friday.
	Summer:	08.00 to 14.00 Monday to Friday.

Currency
Tunisian dinar (D) divided into 1,000 millimes (m).
No Tunisian currency may be taken into or out of Tunisia. Foreign currency unrestricted. To exchange currency at the border, first obtain an exchange slip from a Tunisian bank. Exchange limited to 30 per cent of foreign currency originally exchanged or 100 dinars, whichever is the greater.

Customs
200 cigarettes and one litre alcohol duty free.
General
Population: 5·2 million (1971). 65 per cent agriculture. High unemployment. National income: £90 pa.
British Embassy: 5 Place de la Victoire,
                  Tunis. Telephone: 245 100.

Tunisia gained independence from France in 1956, some French investment remains.

Religion: Moslem, mostly Sunnis. Most mosques are open to non-Muslims.
Official language: Arabic, with much French.
Good road system. Main crops: wheat, barley, olives, wine grapes and citrus fruits.

Visas and inoculations

	Visa	Yellow fever	Smallpox	Cholera	TAB
Algeria	No		Yes		
Chad	Yes	Yes	Yes	Yes	
Libya	Yes		Yes	Yes	
Mali	Yes	Yes	Yes	Yes	
Mauretania	Yes	Yes	Yes	Yes	Yes
Morocco	No	Yes	Yes	Yes	Yes
Niger	Yes	Yes	Yes	Yes	
Spanish Sahara	Yes	Yes	Yes	Yes	
Tunisia	No *		Yes		Yes

* under 2 months

Algeria: Visa and passport regulations change. Consult Passport Office, Clive House, Petty France, London SW1H 9HD. 01-222 8010.

Chad: To obtain visa apply in person to French Consulate, 24 Rutland Gate, London between 10.00 and 15.00 hours, Monday to Friday, with passport, 2 photographs and fee.

Libya: Apply to Libyan Embassy, 58 Princes Gate, London SW7. Visa forms now have to be completed in Arabic, and passport details translated into Arabic. Definitely consult Passport Office before planning visit.

Mali: Visa obtainable only from Malian Embassy in Paris. The visa must be stamped on your passport, but passports cannot be sent by post. Travellers with tour operators should consult them.

Mauritania: Visa obtainable only from Mauritanian Embassy in Paris. See Mali.

Niger: Visa from the French Consulate in London.

Appendix C

Spanish Sahara: Some information obtainable from Spanish Embassy in London but application should be made, in Spanish, to: Direction General de Promocion del Sahara, Vice-Presadencia del Gobierno, Madrid, Spain and three months allowed. Safe conduct pass issued subject to travellers' submission of full details of expedition, route etc. It may be obligatory to take a guide. Hippies, and those without reasonable amounts of money are forbidden entry.

Appendix D

Tourist information

Algeria: Tourist Office, Time and Life Building, New Bond Street, London W1. 01-493 7494.

Chad: French Consulate, 24 Rutland Gate, London SW7. 01-584 9628.
Or write in French to Embassy, 65 rue des Belles-Feuilles, 75016 Paris. 553 3675; or La Direction Générale du Tourisme, BP 748, Fort-Lamy; or l'Agence Tchad Tourisme, BP 894, Fort-Lamy, République du Tchad.

Libya: Embassy, 58 Princes Gate, London SW7. 01-589 5235.

Mali: Write in French to Embassy, 89 rue du Cherche-Midi, Paris 6. 548 5843.

Mauritania: Write in French to Embassy, 5 rue de Montevideo, Paris 16.

Morocco: Tourist Office, 174 Regent Street, London W1. 01-437 0073.

Niger: French Consulate, 24 Rutland Gate, London SW7. 01-584 9628.
Or write in French to Embassy, 154 rue de Longchamps, 75016 Paris. 870 8060.

Tunisia: Tourist Office, 7A Stafford Street, London W1. 01-734 2952.

Spanish Sahara: Write in Spanish to Direction General de Promocion del Sahara, Vice-Presadencia del Gobierno, Madrid, Spain.

Snake and scorpion sera suppliers

Anti-snake serum can be supplied by Hoechst Pharmaceuticals, Hoechst House, Salisbury Road, Hounslow, Middlesex. Ask for 'North Africa Anti-Snake Venom Serum Set'. Price: £10. Life: 3 years.

Anti-scorpion venom serum can be supplied by John Bell & Croydon Limited, 50 Wigmore Street, London W1. Effective against all varieties of scorpion.

General

The Rover Company Limited,
Service Department,
Solihull, Warwickshire.
Telephone: 021-743 4242

The Rover Company Limited,
Parts Department,
PO Box 79,
Cardiff.
Telephone: Cardiff 33681

Volkswagen GB Limited,
Brighton Road,
Purley, Surrey.
Telephone: Purley 4100

Expedition Supplies Limited,
208 Old Brompton Road,
London SW5.
Telephone: 01-370 6677

Black & Edgington Limited,
Ruxley Corner,
Sidcup, Kent.
Telephone: 01-302 0211

Tarpaulin & Tent Mnfg Co,
101 Brixton Hill,
London SW2.
Telephone: 01-674 0121

French Line,
20 Cockspur Street,
London SW1.
Telephone: 01-839 9040

Italian General Shipping Limited,
35 St James's Street,
London SW1.
Telephone: 01-930 6083

British Federation of Sand and Land Yacht Clubs,
c/o Sergeant Major Trevor Spurr,
Tactics Wing,
Royal School of Artillery,
Larkhill,
Salisbury, Wiltshire.

K. Tremble,
Kedek Sheet Metal Company,
97 Felpham Way,
Bognor Regis,
Sussex.

Sand-yacht builders

Gérard Pennel,
Terre plein de l'Ancienne Ecluse
   Guillain,
59 Dunkerque,
France.

Pierre Demoury,
8 rue du Grand Bail,
59 Douai,
France.

Mail

Mail sent Poste Restante from the UK should be given generous time in which to arrive. Services, particularly to Algeria, are not entirely reliable. Algeria: 4 days; Djanet: 8 days; Kano: 6 days; Marrakesh: 5 days; Tamanrasset: 10 days; Tunis: 4 days.

Maps

Michelin series obtainable from leading stationers; price 40p.
Ministry of Defence, Series 2201, obtainable from The Map House, 67 St James's Street, London SW1 or Edward Stanford Limited, 12 Long Acre, London WC2; price approximately 40p each.
Institut Geographique National, 136B rue de Grenelle, Paris VII; price approximately £1 each.
Daily Telegraph Map of Africa, from *Daily Telegraph*, 135 Fleet Street, London EC4; price 25p.

Appendix E

The Rover Company do not have any second-hand vehicles available for sale or hire. However, the following Rover distributors generally have a number of good used Land-Rovers for sale.

Aberdeen	Rossleigh Ltd
Ayr	James Tweedie Ltd
Barnstaple	The County Garage
Basingstoke	Steels (Basingstoke) Ltd
Belfast	Forshaw Automobiles Ltd
Belfast	Charles Hurst Ltd
Birmingham 25	R. H. Collier & Co Ltd
Bournemouth	Stanbourne Motor Co Ltd
Bradford	Albert Farnell Ltd
Brighton 1	Moore of Brighton (1924) Ltd
Bristol 8	Windmill & Lewis Ltd
Bury St Edmunds	Mann Egerton & Co Ltd
Cambridge	Wallis & Son Ltd
Canterbury	Barretts Automobiles Ltd
Cardiff	Morsmith Motors (Cardiff) Ltd
Carlisle	S.M.T. Sales & Service Co Ltd
Carmarthen	Howell's Garage (Carmarthen) Ltd
Chelmsford	Eastern Automobiles Ltd
Cheltenham	Lex Head (Cheltenham) Ltd
Chester	James Edwards (Chester) Ltd
Chesterfield	Cavendish Motors Ltd
Chichester	Chichester Automobiles Ltd
Coventry	Henlys (Coventry) Ltd
Crawley	Southern Counties Garages Ltd
Derby	Mann Egerton & Co Ltd
Dorchester	Dorchester Motor Co Ltd
Dumfries	Dumfries Motor Co Ltd
Dundee	Rossleigh Ltd
Dunsfold, Guildford	Dunsfold Land-Rovers Ltd
Eastbourne	Clark & Lambert Ltd
Edinburgh	Rossleigh Ltd.
Exeter	Motor Macs (Exeter) Ltd
Glasgow W2	Appleyard Gibbon Ltd
Gloucester	Westgate Motor House Co (Gloucester) Ltd
Grimsby	Whites of Grimsby Ltd
Guernsey	St Peter Port Garages
Harrogate	Appleyard of Harrogate Ltd

Appendix E

Haverfordwest	Cartlett Motors Ltd
Huddersfield	W. H. Atkinson & Co (Huddersfield) Ltd
Hull	Gordon Armstrong (Hull) Ltd
Inverness	Inverness Motor Co
Ipswich	Mann Egerton & Co Ltd
Isle of Man	Mylchreests Motors Ltd
Jersey CI	St Helier Garages
Kendal	H. J. Croft
King's Lynn	Mann Egerton (Johnsons) Ltd
Kirkcaldy	Rossleigh Ltd
Leeds 2	Arnold G. Wilson
Leicester	Walter E. Sturgess & Sons Ltd
Lincoln	J. R. J. Mansbridge
Liverpool	C. A. Britten & Co (Liverpool) Ltd
London NW1	Henlys Ltd
Luton	Dunham & Haines Ltd
Maidstone	Miles (Maidstone) Ltd
Manchester 8	David Rosenfield Ltd
Mansfield	James Windsor & Son (Mansfield) Ltd
Newcastle-on-Tyne 2	Rossleigh Ltd
Newport	Dovey Motor Co (Newport) Ltd
Northampton	Grose Westonia Ltd
Norwich	Mann Egerton & Co Ltd
Nottingham	C. H. Truman & Co Ltd
Oxford	Eyles & Coxeter Ltd
Penzance	Taylors (Garage) Ltd
Peterborough	Murkett Bros Ltd
Plymouth	Evans & Cutler (Plymouth) Ltd
Reading	T. Baker & Sons (Reading) Ltd
Rhyl	Brookes Bros (North Wales) Ltd
Ripon	Glovers of Ripon Ltd
Salisbury	Collett's Avon Motors Ltd
Sheffield	Crabtree & Nicol Ltd
Southampton	Steels (Southampton) Ltd
Stirling	Rossleigh Ltd
Stockton-on-Tees	Fred Dinsdale Ltd
Stoke-on-Trent	Byatts of Fenton Ltd
Swansea	Morsmith Motors (Swansea) Ltd
Taunton	Somerset Motors Ltd
Telford	V G Vehicles (Telford) Ltd
Trowbridge	Hebden Knee Motors Ltd

Truro	S. Hicks & Son Ltd
Torquay	South Devon Garages Ltd
Tunbridge Wells	Stevensons Motors Ltd
Windsor	Windsor Motor Co Ltd
Wolverhampton	Hewitts Garages Ltd
Worcester	W. Holloway & Son Ltd

Land-Rover hire

Land-Roving Ltd, 30 Sidbury, Worcester. Telephone 0905 26988
Roverhire, 12 Seagrave Road, London SW6. Telephone 01-385 5291

Rover distributors and dealers in Saharan countries

ALGERIA
Sonacome,
Division Commerciale
   Vehicules,
140 Rue Hassiba Ben Bouali,
Algiers
Postal address: PO Box No 7,
Alger, Belcourt
Telephone:66-41-60/64,66-41-80/84
Distributor for cars and Land-Rovers

CHAD (REPUBLIC OF)
SCOA Automobile Dept,
Rue Paul Levy,
BP 74,
Fort Lamy
Distributor for Land-Rovers only

LIBYA
Tibesti Company Ltd,
PO Box 50,
Benghazi

Tibesti Company Ltd,
Sciara Abuharida,
PO Box 341,
Tripoli
Dealers for cars and Land-Rovers

MALI (REPUBLIC OF)
Manutention Africaine SA,
Boite Postale 143,
Bamako
Telephone: 229-57
Distributor for Land-Rovers only

MAURETANIA (ISLAMIC REPUBLIC OF)
Compagnie Technique
Mauretanienne (Cotema)
313 Nouakchott
Telephone: 22-53
Distributor for Land-Rovers only

MOROCCO
Aetco-Lever-Maroc,
47 Boulevard Ba Hamad,
Boite Postale 519,
Casablanca
Telephone: 418-71 to 73, 426-91 to
92; 430-83 to 85
Distributor for cars and Land-Rovers

NIGER (REPUBLIC OF)
Niger Afrique,
Boite Postale 62,
Niamey
Telephone: 3038/9
Distributor for Land-Rovers only

Appendix E

SPANISH SAHARA
Metalurgica de Santa Ana, SA,
Delegacion En El Aaiun,
Apartado 8,
El Aaiun
Distributor for Land-Rovers only

TUNISIA
Le Moteur, SA,
54 Avenue de Carthage,
Tunis
Telephone: 242.166
Distributor for cars and Land-Rovers

Appendix F

List of tools suggested by Rover Company for expeditionary purposes. Some additional suggestions are added beneath the list.

Wheel brace

Double lifting jack, shaft and handle

Tyre pump, hand operated

Tyre pressure gauge

Grease and oil gun

Starting handle

Tool roll

Combination pliers

Screwdriver, ⅜in blade, 9⅜in long, Standard and Phillips

Spanner, ³⁄₁₆in × ¼in Whitworth

Spanner, ⁵⁄₁₆in × ⁷⁄₁₆in Whitworth

Spanner, single-ended, ⅜in Whitworth

Spanner, ⁵⁄₁₆in × ⅜in AF (bleed screw for DPA pump, diesel only)

Spanner, ⁷⁄₁₆in × ½in AF

Spanner, ¹¹⁄₁₆in × ¾in AF

Spanner, ⅝in × ⁹⁄₁₆in AF

6in adjustable spanner, large, 1⅛in adjustment

Sparking plug spanner and extension (petrol models only)

Box spanner

Tommy bar

Set of socket spanners (good quality)

Electrical screwdriver

Pin punch

Feeler gauges, 0·015in to 0·025in

Hammer, 1lb

Large 'Mole grips'

Chisel

Small magnet with bar

Hand drill with bits

Inspection lamp and extension lead

12in rule

2 Hacksaws and spare blades—

1 small   1 large

10in flat file, smooth and rough

10in round file, smooth and rough

Box spanner, 1⅛in × 1¼in Whitworth

Oil can

Box of assorted nuts and bolts, screws and jubilee clips

Length of electrical wire and electrical connectors

Large flat metal drip tray for mechanical repairs

Long-nose pliers

Roll of electrical insulation tape

Roll of masking tape

3 tyre levers: large

Puncture repair outfit and spare inner tubes

Hydraulic jack

Standard jack

Flat plates to support jack on soft ground

Axe

Additions

Crowbar

1in paint brush

Ball of string

Small vice (mounted on bumper)

Large soldering iron, solder and flux

Emery cloth

Sidecutters

Schrader spark plug pump

Roll of general-purpose wire

Hub nut spanner

Vehicle manual

Jump lead

Assorted washers

Appendix F

List of spares recommended for Land-Rovers.

Rear spring complete
Front spring main leaf
Shackle bolts (2 of each kind)
'U' bolts and nuts
Spring bushes
Shock absorber rubbers
Half shaft rear LH
Half shaft rear RH
Driving member rear
Driving member front
Several hub oil seals
Petrol pump complete with sediment bowl
Brake flexible hoses
Fan belts
Spark plugs
Distributor cap and plug leads
Decarbonising gasket set
Contact sets
Ignition coil
Condenser
Rotor arm
Oil filter element
Top water hose
Bottom water hose
Fuses
Bulbs
Brake fluid

Grease
Clutch slave-cylinder kit
Brake wheel-cylinder kits
Hub bearing inner
Hub bearing outer
Axle drain plugs
Axle check straps
Speedometer cable inner
Jubilee clips
Assorted split pins
Dynamo brushes
Radiator cap
Gasket paper
Workshop manual
'Araldite' kit
Water pump, complete
Petrol pump repair kit
Differential/axle case gaskets
Glass sediment bowl for fuel pump
Clutch pin for operating shaft
8ft length Bundy brake tubing with male and female nuts
Tin of radiator seal

Diesel Land-Rovers only
2 injectors and sealing rings
2 heater plugs
2 fuel filters

Appendix G

Atlas Expeditions Limited, 45 Beauchamp Place, Knightsbridge, London SW3. 01-589 9411.

Encounter Overland Limited, 1 Munro Terrace, London SW10. 01-352 3702. Overland expeditions from London to Johannesburg scheduled to take 13 weeks, 4 departures a year both directions. Saharan section is Laghouat to Zinder (16 days) via the main trans-Saharan *piste* (Ain Salah, Taman-rasset, Agadés). Transport used are 3-ton four-wheel drive 18-person Bedford trucks. 7 years experience of which 4 are on this route. Inclusive price for the one-way trip about £400.

Hughes Overland, 14 Exchange Way, Chelmsford, Essex. 0245 65501. Air London-Malaga, overland Malaga-Marrakesh-Gaulimine-Agadir; 15 days, 9 departures: about £80 inclusive. Mainly young people. Travel by 15-seat Ford Transit Minibus. Also air to Tunis, 15 days tour in Tunisia and Algeria; 11 departures: about £80 inclusive.

Intertrek Limited, 62 Battersea High Street, London SW11. 01-228 0498. Overland London-Nairobi, Mediterranean crossing to Tunis, Eastern Sahara via Djanet to Agadés (exact route not specified). Young people (18 to 35) only; 18 seats in Bedford truck. 3 departures per year each direction, 11 weeks, about £450 largely inclusive.

Jerrycan, 53 rue du Stand, 1204-Geneva, Switzerland. (022) 216011. Air Geneva-Algiers-Tamanrasset. Overland Tamanrasset-Djanet. Air Djanet-Algiers. 18 days. 4 departures a year in both directions. Camel and walking sidetrips to see rock paintings in both Hoggar and Tassili regions. Also 15-day air-land cruises in Southern Morocco. Vehicles are 14-seat Ford trucks and 9-seat Land-Rovers, seat capacities reduced for Saharan tours. Specific aim is to produce non-tour atmosphere. Inclusive prices around £375 for Sahara, £225 for Morocco. Also Air Geneva-Djanet, group of 12 with 24 Méhari camels travel a circuit of 150 miles, taking 2 weeks: object is to gain a feel of the desert. 2 departures, about £300.

Penn Overland Tours Limited, 122 Knightsbridge, London SW1X 7PG. 01-589 0016. Air London-Algiers, overland Algiers-Nairobi, via trans-Saharan *piste*, Tamanrasset, Agadés (19 days in Saharan section), 4 departures each way. From £303. Also 2 and 3 weeks Morocco Airtreks from £90; 2 weeks Tunisian Exploration Airtrek from £94; 4 weeks Morocco, Algeria and Tunisia Airtrek from £155; 3 weeks Roman Africa and Sahara Airtrek from £125; 6 weeks Great North Africa overland from Belgium from £169. Vehicles Range-Rovers and Afrikabuses.

Appendix G

Quest 4, Ashton Wold, Peterborough, Huntingdon. Oundle 2614. Expedition consultants. Land-Rover, Bedford truck vehicles and drivers available for charter for all Saharan expeditionary work.

Rene Dee Expeditions Limited, Aqua House, 24 Old Steine, Brighton, Sussex. Brighton 681523. Air London-Agadir, camel expedition in Southern Morocco and overland in Ford 15-seat Minibus; 3 weeks, 8 departures, about £195.

Siafu Expeditions Limited, 18 Dawes Road, Fulham, London SW6 7EN. 01-381 1388/1439. Air from London to Tunis, overland Tunis to Nairobi expeditions scheduled to take 12 weeks, 13 departures a year in both directions. London to Kano (5 weeks) may also be booked. Saharan section is subject to variation but keeps, in principle, to the eastern routes using local guides between Djanet and Agadés. Vehicles are Bedford trucks and Land-Rovers which may be passenger driven. Also offer specialist expeditions to Sahara. Price, largely inclusive, about £450.

Tentrek Expeditions Limited, Station Approach, Chislehurst, Kent. 01-467 3473. Rail-ferry to Paris, overland via France, Spain, Ceuta, Marrakesh, Ouazazate, 16 days, 33 departures, about £50 non-inclusive; 3 weeks, 29 departures, about £60 non-inclusive; 4 weeks, 3 departures, about £80. Mainly for young people, travel by Ford 15-seat Minibus.

Appendix H

APPENDIX H: SUGGESTED READING

Across the Sahara (1910) (account of slave trade) — Hanns Vischer
Across the Sahara by Motor Car (1924) — G. M. Haardt and Laudouin-Dubreuil

Africa Handbook (covers all Africa) — Colin Legum
*The Great Sahara (the history of the Sahara) — J. Wellard
History of the Arabs (1942) (the rise of Islam) — Phillip K. Hitti
Memoirs of the Foreign Legion (1924) — Maurice Magnus
Sahara — John Julius Norwich
*Sahara (1970) (general description; superbly illustrated) — René Gardi
Le Sahara Francais — Capot-Rey
Sahara, The Great Desert (1935) (translation of French classic) — E. F. Gautier
The Search for the Tassili Frescoes (1959) (an account of the paintings) — Henri Lhote
Travels and Discoveries in North and Central Africa (1890) (a classic now out of print) — Dr Henry Barth
*The Tuareg — Ken and July Slavia

*Particularly recommended

Acknowledgements

In compiling this book I have to acknowledge my debt to many Saharan travellers whose advice and help has always been given unstintingly. In any event, I know the names of but few of those who, without a second thought, stepped into the breach whenever the need arose. Neither would these travellers expect mention—their actions were spontaneous and in accordance with the tradition of the desert. My acknowledgement is therefore to this tradition and to those who uphold it.

I should like to mention specifically the help I have received from Jim Page who has kindly vetted the entire manuscript and also compiled from his own comprehensive experience the list of Land-Rover spare parts.

I would also like to record the substantial and efficient co-operation which I have received from Herbert Sylge, lately of Minitrek Ltd. I am also indebted to him for illustrations Nos 1, 2, 4, 9, 10, 11, 13, 15, 16, 26, 29, 30, 32, 33, 35, 36, 37 as well as the colour photograph on the dust jacket which illustrates an expedition setting off for the interior.